Level Up:

The Best Kept Secrets to Overcoming Roadblocks, Achieving Success & Multiplying Results

© 2021 by Double Agent Marketing LLC
Robert Plank & Lance Tamashiro
(408) 277-0904

Introduction

What-if's. Concern about what others think. Trouble letting go of the past regrets and mistakes.

Wherever you are in life now -- second marriage, third career, or starting over in business for the fourth time, mistakes are proof that you're trying!

When you were younger, did you learn about the process of a caterpillar transforming into a butterfly? It's easy to forget that in the MIDDLE of that entire process, this creature is in "chrysalis" form -- an ugly, gooey, messy sack. In other words, if you feel like a pile of goo right now, keep going.

Reaching your next goal and making progress often requires that you drop old bad habits and behaviors for something new.

> *"Every next level of your life will demand a different you."* -- Leonardo Dicaprio

However, it can be tough to go it alone, especially with self-doubt, a lack of support system, and uncertainty. That's why I've found a group of successful people to inform and share how they have "levelled up" -- in their own way. Enjoy!

Level 1: Leadership... Create Change Using Your Open Playbook by Larry Dodd

How do YOU change? More importantly, how do you inspire change in others, perhaps in your organization? Spreadsheets, flowcharts, process, other tools of change? Those are critical elements to this "change" process, but the most foundational is: building the RELATIONSHIP which underlies and supports the trust required to execute these tools of change. I developed a three-step process called OpenPlaybook™ -- that drives effective leadership to successfully execute these processes.

The Three Pillars of Change

There is consistent pressure in business to change. The consequences of you NOT changing are high: it opens up opportunities for your competitors to gain ground. You might miss critical game-changing shifts in the marketplace that place your organization in peril. To successfully compete in the world of business, change should be a daily process. Leaders are charged with leading organizations and the people who serve them through this process on a daily basis. I highly suggest you consider developing these three "playbooks" in order to make change happen:

1. **The Playbook You Were Given.** Know yourself. Do your homework. Understand your built-in skills, talents, and temperaments. Offer what no one else offers, your authentic self. Always do the homework on yourself to continuously improve your game.

2. **The Playbook You'll Create and Develop.** Once you've developed a discipline of doing the homework on yourself, think about the change process that you are seeking to implement. Your competitive advantage is being able to see others clearly because you have a clear handle on yourself and what you have to offer that no one else can. You have developed the consistent discipline of always developing your own playbook (the one you were given) which empowers you to build an authentic bridge to those you are seeking to develop through change. You too are walking a path of consistent growth. This will build trust because you are leading by example.

3. **The Playbook You Give Away.** Consider who you will give your authentic playbook to and why. Choose carefully. Build the right people for the circumstances at hand and your change initiatives will far outstrip whatever vision you have for success.

The Playbook You Were Given works within the same swim lane as your skills, talents, and temperaments. These attributes always existed within you. However, outside factors, the "shoulds" -- get in the way. I "should" make this much money, have this job title and do this job.

Those "should's" are the contents of someone else's playbook. You may think that THEIR playbook should be YOUR playbook, not because of your skills and talents, but because of your ideas about what their playbook will give you. The result is often frustration, disillusionment, bad behavior, and breakdown.

What is YOUR playbook? Question everything, especially the whispers of purpose you have drowned out with everyone else's "should's." Ask yourself these questions:

- What do you lean toward?

- Are you a people person?

- Do you like facts and figures?

- How do you best absorb information?

- What do you think about when you compare yourself to other people?

- Do you see strengths or do you see weaknesses?

As a change maker, I find and invest in people who are ready to awaken, believe, and take RISKS!

> *"He who looks outside, dreams.*
> *He who looks INSIDE, awakens."*
> *-- Carl Jung*

Issues arise when you find the inherent strengths you offer, and develop those into productive contributions, on individual and team levels.

Working on **The Playbook I Was Given**, I discovered my inherent strengths: making change, building people, seeing the strengths (which they needed in specific situations) and turning those people into productive teams. How does this relate to what YOU may be missing in your career or business?

The Key to Success: Getting the Right People, in the Right Place, with the Right Attitude, At the Right Time

Some people are better suited for a specific change than others.

I worked in accounting for a large public home builder. I was completely frustrated. My own "change" (and growth) had stopped. Contemplating a career change, I consulted a career counselor. After taking the Myers-Briggs personality assessment, I discovered my temperaments were the opposite of most typical accountants. This encouraged me to fully explore, understand and utilize the playbook.

Within a month, I discovered a wonderful niche in the business arena that few accounting and finance professionals could serve: the skills, talents, and temperament that not only welcomed BUT thrived on change. In situations where change was necessary, I was the "shiny rock." That knowledge led me to a wonderful career with a unique niche.

I needed to refocus to find the right role for me, and once I centered myself, it gave me a level of authenticity that attracted the right situation. I gained the confidence to know exactly what I was looking for in an organization, which positioned me to be a good fit. I became the right person, in the right place, with the right attitude, at the right time. It worked for me and will work for you.

My path led to a career-changing experience with a newly acquired major league baseball team. They wanted change, and I was hired to provide it. Had I not done the homework shortly before this opportunity, I would have never found the confidence I needed. This journey has led me to train people to speak in front of audiences, build others up, communicate, and LEAD in a positive way. This developed as a result of the natural progression of one logical step after the next, based on the belief that, every day, I understood myself a little better.

The biggest mistake when making change: lack of self-knowledge and the resulting authenticity to develop people based on TRUST. Consider those times you observe talents (skills) in others in your team, that the person may not know they possess! That person needs your acknowledgment so that your team will benefit. You need to build trust to overcome these obstacles. People trust you more when they know and trust themselves.

The Closer You Get to a Natural, Authentic State of Who You Are, the More Frightening It Becomes...and the More You Grow!

Through creating a confidence base under the tables and flowcharts, you find people to develop because you can hear the whispers of change. Building confidence empowers you to leverage your creativity, then help people see and believe in their potential.

This is the thinking and thought process I take leaders through. Leadership is about leading people to seek out those changes from the beginning. The magical part is that after a while, those changes look for YOU. Authenticity breeds trust, which leads to growth.

Think about the interactions you have with others. When you lack confidence, others are not confident in you. You're not authentic and people question your authority. Your uncertain self is not your best self. Intuitively, others sense that in you. Conversely, you show increased confidence and strength in building relationships when you come from self-knowledge. You know who you are and what you have to give. "Coax out" the hidden talents of other people. You inspire them to share, often for the first time, their strengths and abilities.

Years ago, I was hired as a Chief Financial Officer to drive change in a rapidly growing organization. A very smart senior accountant worked under me. He easily answered any question I asked of him. He was ready to grow. I built a relationship with him and challenged him with new, outside-the-box projects. I explained the "why" of what we were doing. I didn't know his growth path, but I knew it existed. I listened to his story and heard the whispers of strength that only trust can present. A few months later, an Accounting Manager position opened up. He was ready for the challenge. He was confident enough to step up. He trusted the process even if he didn't know the exact outcome because he trusted me as a leader.

He didn't know how powerful he was in the beginning! After two years, we moved him two levels "up" in the organization.

The Playbook You Create focuses on preparing and executing the obvious changes you want to make. It provides a clear roadmap detailing where to go, how to get there, and what it looks like when you get there. If your self-development behaviors regularly show this, you are better positioned to improve others. Developing others means you ask them to change, do something different, embrace a new idea or new process. This risk requires them to trust their leader, YOU!

Change is Frightening: Get Comfortable Being Uncomfortable

As a leader who was developing my own playbook, I improve myself and lead by example at the same time. I inspire others to step towards a daunting target, so they will be much more likely to go in the direction I need them to go. By continuing to develop, I show them by example why growth requires "getting comfortable being uncomfortable." This is a key part of the growth process and a cornerstone of strong leaders.

The Playbook You Develop is important because if I'm driving a change initiative for an organization by working through people, I must create a compelling vision that illustrates where I want us to be when we finish, what the finish line looks and feels like. I have to consistently live it. To accomplish this, I paint a vivid word picture, and work in every moment to bring that to life. Clarity of goals and consistency of action conquer fear.

Two time-tested "organizational change" principles always play out: One, as a leader, if we finish the change initiative and it looks exactly like the picture I painted, I've failed. Two, my ultimate goal is to find a leader to step up and make the end result BETTER than my picture, to drive the organization further. He or she becomes the leader I develop.

When I develop this playbook, I develop the people to lead, own, and improve the process. The idea unleashes what they know about the business, and what they learn about what they offer. They take it further than I ever could envision.

With the right foundation of trust, the right people move through fear to literally move mountains!

Your playbook is the way you do the business of being you.

Imagine a six-month change initiative, for example, converting to a new computer system. The temptation is to think that the system conversion is about putting in a new computer system. It is not! A successful system conversion requires people to rethink how the organization works, from the ground up: be open to change, new roles, and better deliverables. In this scenario, the change initiative is "technically" complete, after six months. However, if you haven't changed the underlying processes, attitudes, and commitments (the culture), you have the same problem in a prettier box.

Change occurs in the hearts of people. That new computer system is the instrument of change, not the change itself.

When you change the culture of an organization, you change the heartbeat of that organization, the way people view their job, how they do their job, how they interact with others, what success looks like, and why. You move the needle. This is a journey, not a destination. Leaders are compelled to continually think about how to improve, how to build people, who we build, and why.

We, leaders, should drive constant innovation. If you allow your organization and teams to stand still, then you're falling behind. Business is a competitive environment, as it should be! It challenges you to be slightly better today than yesterday. It requires creative thought and continuous improvement.

Leadership is a muscle. If you're a weightlifter, lifting weights is a process. It becomes your way of doing things over time. You become stronger and healthier as a result. This same discipline applies to organizations, especially when creating something different. The organization is always going forward as it builds a culture that supports the ideals that motivates people and positively builds them.

What are your YOUR true strengths and abilities? **What do you offer?** How can you advance those skills and learn to trust the process? It's easy to get stuck. I know firsthand! I struggled with these exact issues during the first eight years of my career. The frustration of self-discovery moved me into the next level.

Self-Discovery Through Frustration

Prior to the "big break" in my career of working for a Major League Baseball Club, I was completely frustrated. I made my boss and co-workers unhappy. I couldn't survive and reached out for help.

I leveled up from the point of complete frustration into having a vision. Within months, I enjoyed the biggest break in my career -- that was the big-league baseball team opportunity in which I was tasked, along with the rest of the acquisition management team, with leading change in a high-profile environment. It was a career-maker. I was prepared because I "did the work."

Assessment tools such as Myers-Briggs and CliftonStrengths by Gallup are starting points. The work you do AROUND them is what's valuable. Use those results to provide a proven framework in order to develop better questions about yourself that only you can actually answer.

The currency of a leader is TIME. We never have enough! Spend it wisely.

"Choice" Is Essential

The third and final pillar: give away your playbook. Give away your experience. It takes time to give away your experience to someone who has not traveled as far down the path. It is critical to realize that you're giving away what no one else can offer but you. Invest your time wisely. Be careful how you spend it and why. Choose the right people to take advantage of the experience and contribute to your team's success.

Companies use many strategies to convince good employees to stay. More money, more perks, free meals, more tangible material "things." These things are easily replicable by others. Employing this type of leadership undermines your team by commoditizing your value proposition by giving what everyone else can also give. This builds a team of mercenaries who are likely to jump at the next better deal.

The things that a leader has to offer which nobody else can are their experience, their heart, and their passion... those are the things which lead to teams of committed people. They can't be offered by anybody else because nobody else lived them. The leader did. If you interact with a key employee you are developing, the chances of success will be much higher, and so will your ability to serve both that employee and the company when you invest in them. Giving your playbook away to them.

Change starts at the top, with the leader. People hear what you say but follow what they see authentically lived. Model the right things and the right values to get the right foundation to successfully make improvements. Use these three pillars to take the company where it needs to go.

Have you opened YOUR playbook? What are you doing with it? Are you actively developing it and strategic plans for your team? Are you listening to the whispers of strength in others? Are you purposefully giving your playbook away to the people that you are developing? Have you selected those people wisely? Do you have the right leaders in the right place with the right attitude at the right time? If you do, are THEY building THEIR people in the same way? Do they know who they're building and why? Do they have the right approach to building people? Do they have the right playbook? Are they giving away their playbook? Are they developing their people?

How can you know? Frequently you'll see it happen in the later hours of the day or over lunch or at a time when it's inconvenient because this is when it's convenient for the organization. This is an important way to measure the hearts of the people you develop. How far are they willing to reach?

If your organization is striving to make change through people by building on strengths, an OpenPlaybook™ will help. When you have an open playbook, you build trust, lead with authenticity, develop yourself, and others. In creating the playbook you have provided, designing the playbook in tandem with driving key improvement strategies and giving away the playbook selectively, your organization's development and the growth of the key people in it will be absolutely stunning. This

OpenPlaybook™ strategy has driven success in my career. It will work for you.

*Larry Dodd from **Open-Playbook.com** is a keynote speaker and thought leader around strengths-based leadership. He challenges you to combine the best of what your team has to contribute with the appropriate management tools for where you are and then trains you to master them. This takes you from where you are to where you need to go, building a results-driven, people-first culture that consistently exceeds expectations.*

- Website: **www.Open-Playbook.com**

- Cell Phone: **925-448-4122**

Level 2: Authority... Become the In-Demand Celebrity in Your Industry by Larry Becht

Do you believe that you were destined for something greater? Are you sometimes terrified of "getting comfortable in mediocre-land" and yet, with family and other commitments, you fear you have too much on your plate to put in the time and effort to build your business and your legacy?

If so, then you can relate to Dr. Martin. A dentist at a large dental practice with five other dentists, he always dreamed of opening his own practice. It would take planning, time, and resources. Recently married with his first baby on the way, he couldn't afford to fail, or even struggle. With many well-known, established dentists in his city, he knew it might take years to build his practice with a consistent flow of patients.

The large corporate dental clinics and famous dentists were everywhere on TV, Radio, Billboards, and the Internet. They had huge marketing and advertising budgets. Dr. Martin wanted to provide for his family

AND compete with these "big fish" at the same time. Authority Marketing was his answer.

There has never been a more important time to establish YOUR Authority. Now is the time to build a successful business and get your message out. Don't wait to get "intentional" about building your brand. You'll fall further behind competitors who are out-working you at this very moment.

The first impression most people have of you and your brand no longer happens in person or over the phone. It happens online, via Google, your website, and social media channels. Your brand is what Google says it is!

> *"There is a huge secret about income that only a small percentage of top earners in every field ever figure out and use to their advantage. The secret is that the higher up in income you go, in almost any category, the more you are paid for who you are rather than for what you do."*
>
> *-- Dan Kennedy, Leading Expert on Direct-Response Marketing and Copywriting*

My client Dr. Martin realized that his ability to own the room (by itself) would not be enough to succeed in today's media landscape. His degrees mounted on the wall and years of hard-earned experience were "nice" but those things must be intentionally amplified online to ensure that the brand image you project presents you as the Authority you are.

Focus on this marketing. Begin as a thought leader -- NOT the brand -- to make a larger impact:

- When you focus on "corporate branding" you are competing against brands with several decades of a head-start on you. They have more awareness and more money to spend on marketing...

- When people interact with corporate brands, they're expecting to be MARKETED to. When people interact with a thought leader or Authority, they're expecting to LEARN, which dramatically shifts their perspective...

- We've grown distrustful of corporate brands and are instead giving attention to individual thought leaders who we view as unbiased and trustworthy.

Authority = Expertise x Celebrity

Authority occurs when you take the right steps to combine stand-out, trustworthy expertise in your field with "celebrity" high visibility. Your "expert" name becomes synonymous with your field, which provides an incalculable advantage over your competitors.

It's never been easier to build Authority and use it to accelerate the speed of trust with your customers. In today's media environment, driven by discoverability and brand-building pre-engagement, you combine great knowledge and expertise with celebrity-style visibility. You are perceived as more than just "another expert" that someone can price shop against competitors. Instead, you are the go-to thought leader in your field. Any prospect would feel fortunate to even get a meeting with you!

It doesn't just happen to you. This is a specific process called Authority Marketing which builds your visibility and credibility in your field, and uses that thought leadership as a way to drive business and make a bigger impact. This creates an incredibly unfair advantage over your competitors.

It cannot be achieved quietly. You want to be seen as a thought leader in your field, a person of outstanding authority whose observations are accorded instant respect, whose advice is almost treated as a prescription, and makes a positive impact that leaves a lasting legacy.

One of the most powerful ways to achieve this rare stature is through book authorship. But in today's media landscape, the journey to becoming an Authority isn't complete with a book -- that's just the beginning.

If you wish to achieve fame and status in your field, design and implement an Authority Marketing plan that includes multiple strategies -- often INCLUDING book authorship -- to position yourself as an undisputed expert, influential Authority, and in-demand Celebrity.

When you combine stand-out Expertise (which many people have), with the visibility of Celebrity (which some people have), you become an Authority (which few people are). These two factors, working in concert, deliver three desirable benefits: you attract more and better clients, make selling to them easier, and make price less of an issue. The profitability of your business improves!

How do you effectively and efficiently become an Authority? **An Authority Marketing Plan.**

We established Dr. Martin's Authority Marketing Plan, created an online (and offline) strategy to build his Authority. Within a few months, he broke ground on a new building site for his dental practice. With several months of construction ahead, we launched his Plan so he could generate attention, interest, and anticipation for this new practice. The goal was to have patients scheduled and ready for appointments as soon as the doors opened.

> *"The value of firmly establishing your authority in your field cannot be overstated. Sharing your unique perspective within your field is one of the most direct and powerful ways to make this happen. It is your vehicle to drive real and lasting change. People have to know you're there."*
>
> *-- Steve Forbes, Chairman and Editor-in-Chief of Forbes Media*

How to Become an Authority

Effective Authority Marketing involves a strategic process of systematically positioning a persona as the leader and expert in your industry, community, and marketplace to command an outsized influence and edge on your competitors.

An Authority Marketing Plan levels the playing field by focusing on your individual Authority brand. You BECOME your own brand. Today, people are skeptical of large corporate brands. Authority Marketing accelerates your "speed of trust" like nothing else.

You are no longer seen as someone "selling" but instead as a thought leader with something to teach. Use Authority to establish trust before you sit down with someone. When you do this, you don't have to establish your credibility or make the case as to why you're the best resource. Go right to problem solving. As such, people are more willing to take your recommendations.

Authority reduces the sales cycle. Potential clients shop around less, if at all. They feel lucky to talk to you. They choose you because of WHO you are (a trustworthy advisor) rather than WHAT you offer.

Leverage Authority in your industry, community, or marketplace to generate a higher volume of qualified leads, a magnet with leads flowing toward you.

There are three categories of media: Rented, Earned, and Owned...

- **Rented Media:** All media where you fully control the content but you don't own the real estate... including advertising, social media channels (i.e. your LinkedIn account, Facebook page), bio pages on corporate sites, etc. Rented media doesn't provide much Authority because the audience knows the barrier to entry is incredibly low: anyone can buy an ad or start a Twitter account. It doesn't provide targeted access to your audience at scale, leading back to your owned media, where, for the purposes of Authority Marketing, all roads should lead!

- **Earned Media:** All media on real estate you don't own, where the perception of the audience is that you EARNED the media, including publicity, speaking engagements, online reviews, referrals, word-of-mouth, your book, and beyond. Nothing provides more immediate Authority than earned media.

Many people make the mistake of putting all their eggs in this single basket, which is very dangerous, because you don't have direct control over media going out. Think about it: with earned media, you must rely on someone else to do something for your message to spread (i.e. your customer is at the right dinner party next to the right person to make a referral, or the producer who decides to put you on the air)...

- **Owned Media:** This includes any asset where you fully own the connection to your audience, providing you with more leverage than any other category of media, because you own the real estate. Your website, blog, email list, and physical mailing list exist within this category.

These media types feed each other, but when you consider owned media in the context of the new media landscape, the greatest success comes when you intentionally focus on moving your audience from rented and earned media to your OWNED media. The biggest game-changer in Authority Marketing is growing owned media.

An effective Authority Marketing Plan includes optimizing the use of each of these types of media in addition to designing a customized solution for you across these areas:

- Branding and Omnipresence

- Lead Generation

- Content Marketing

- PR & Media

- Speaking

- Events

- Referral Marketing

We utilized all three media types (rented, earned and owned) in Dr. Martin's online and offline Authority Marketing plan.

Online efforts included his new website, rapid gains in search engine rankings due to our efforts with SEO and social media, and pay-per-click advertising for high-value case-specific procedures. His online presence exploded in his area.

Offline, we helped him write and publish his own dentistry book. He is featured in a full-length magazine mailed to thousands of nearby households. He recorded a 30-minute segment to broadcast on his local TV station several times each week. He was featured in daily Rush Limbaugh radio commercials. He realized a significant increase in business with each new layer. He's established Authority in his market in a short time.

> *"The number one key to making yourself a powerful, magnetic, trusted, high-income individual, to any target audience or market, is your known and accepted status as an Authority."*

> *-- Dan Kennedy, Leading Expert on Direct-Response Marketing and Copywriting*

The Path to a More Prosperous and Fulfilling Life

If you want to be liberated from selling, and prescribe rather than sell, build your status and Authority. Become the leader in your field. By establishing yourself as a thought leader, you make your business and yourself a magnet for opportunity.

When you are THE Authority in your field -- the expert when it comes to your product or service -- you must constantly apply yourself and sharpen your sword. Learn, grow, and adapt to the changing marketplace. Committing to be an Authority is a commitment to lifelong learning and growing.

Being the Authority gives you choices, and the more choices you have, the more control you have over your destiny. You're in-demand. You can pick-and-choose which engagements fulfill you. You have more influence. You're a trusted advisor, not a salesperson peddling goods.

The more you become an Authority, the higher level your sphere of influence and the higher-level circles you run in. That results in higher-level relationships, including not only in business, but even those with families and loved ones.

When you become the Authority, it makes you a magnet for opportunity. The more opportunity in your life, the more optimistic you become about the future, and the more you can help others, leading to a more prosperous and fulfilling life!

There has never been a better time than NOW to become an Authority. The power that traditionally belonged to corporate media giants is in the hands of every individual for the benefit of anyone who understands how to use it. By serving others first, you gain an outsized advantage on your competition. You increase the speed of trust with your customers and clients. You leverage success into greater success.

Authority Marketing works because it's customizable, adaptable, and authentic to who you are and what you do. When you become an Authority, people find you. They see you wrote a book on the topic, or read articles you've written. They see you as a trusted source, a knowledgeable insider in your field. They contact you because of your Authority. This changes everything, because the quality of these leads are higher than those from any other type of marketing.

When you become an Authority, you'll realize these benefits:

- Business comes to you because money follows and flows to Authority

- Clients acquire status by having a leading expert working for them

- Experts, professionals, and providers do not sell their recommendations -- they have the Authority needed to PRESCRIBE!

Authority comes from a variety of factors including expert status, environment, customer mind-set, criticality of the solution, and more. The difference in your customer's reaction to a proposed solution to their problem is based on their acceptance of the Authority of the person making the recommendation.

Working with an expert to create and implement your own customized Authority Marketing Plan is KEY for your success.

One year after launching his own practice, Dr. Martin's life is entirely different. He has a steady stream of patients. He continues to build the foundation by investing even more into his marketing efforts. He competes with the big names in his market. He's captured a significant amount of market share. He's experienced single months of revenue that have surpassed his entire previous year's revenue. Most importantly, he has time for family. He and his wife have welcomed their baby boy into the world. He takes Fridays off to enjoy life with them. What began as a dream for Dr. Martin has become a reality using Authority Marketing.

Larry Becht is the Founder of Authority Marketing Experts, an innovative Marketing company helping clients achieve Authority status in their market and exponentially grow their business through online and offline strategies.

Take the Authority Assessment to find out your current authority status. Most industries have plenty of experts, but very few rise to authority status. Visit AuthorityMarketingExperts.com/assessment to get your results immediately. Then, take the next steps to get started with your own Authority Marketing Plan by scheduling your complimentary Authority Strategy Session today!

Level 3: Prospecting... Create a Local Media Asset to Land Clients by Drew Griffin

A HUGE local marketing shift occurred just a few years ago. I was struggling to connect with local businesses. I knew about search engine optimization, website development, app development, social postings, and blog writing, but business owners were NOT interested in our services!

The clients we had been serving for years noticed new options. They considered moving to other agencies offering similar services, sometimes at a major discount. We asked ourselves, what was the path forward? Undercut our competitors, differentiate offerings, add value, or BE DIFFERENT?

My business partner (David Calafiore) and I faced a harsh reality. We couldn't continue to offer that same service and expect different results. Something had to change.

The Problem Solver's Mindset

How did I get here? I worked as a hyperbaric wound care nurse for 25 years. The iPhone sparked my curiosity. Patients found it difficult to control their blood sugar. I noticed an opportunity to assist patients using technology. I developed one of the first apps to help diabetics track blood glucose. At that time, people were new to the "app" concept, but we had a trending product, with 30,000 downloads after a couple of weeks. I realized the potential to reach more people with this emerging, exciting, rapidly expanding technology. We were one of the pioneers.

I was inspired by the idea of leveling up and escaping the clinic. I could reach people differently through internet marketing. I developed an app but had to learn effective marketing strategies to reach customers on Facebook.

Working in the medical industry for 25 years, I noticed the same outstanding issue. Many people struggled managing diabetes. Everyday, diabetics made the same mistakes (making decisions based on limited information) dosing the wrong amount of insulin. How would I change the lives of newly diagnosed patients?

This new app allowed a diabetic patient to journal, record blood sugar trends, and as a result, modify their diets and activities. I could only help a limited number of patients per hour. This mobile tool helped communicate their daily patterns to their physician and care team. The process: developing the concept, learning the language, programming, finding help from others, marketing it, was an interesting change in my life's direction. We identified a problem we could solve in a unique way.

How Do YOU Differentiate Yourself and Your Business?

Now that you understand my process, I'd like to explain how we transitioned away from being just a "local marketing agency" -- because it can help with your own thought process and problem solving. We were common -- comparable with others. We observed with agency owners who didn't know what they were doing but were good salespeople, bold enough to ask for a discount. Even today, many people advertise on Facebook -- they know how to sell a product but don't know how to get the result the customer wants.

Challenges are everywhere, for both you and me. It costs nothing to make a business card and tell people you are in business. We call these "Me-Too Agencies." Each person is the same as everyone else, saying, "I offer SEO, WordPress, blogging."

We had a decision to make. We wanted to sell ourselves differently, and created a framework that markets using attention.

Could larger companies offer a cheaper or more robust service? How would we survive when everyone else offered identical services? How could we break away from the customer merry-go-round?

Change the Local Marketing Game

In your own situation, how would you compete against a sea of local marketers (or established companies) with extensive databases, capital, and resources? What if, instead, customers approached YOU, because YOU had all the attention? Imagine that you, a marketer or agency owner who wanted to differentiate, approached a local business owner, and asked ONE of the following two possible questions?

Option #1: "We'd like to SELL a service to you, and it will bring you attention." (the old way)

Option #2: "We would love to feature you on the cover of our magazine. We want to learn more about your book, software, and your business."

Which option would your ideal client choose? Instead of being sold, that business owner would rather appear on your magazine cover and talk about themselves. This is a simple way to build a "link." Create your own "media company" based around local news and events. You can effectively compete against major media companies, newspapers, and television stations. You can be quicker in delivering the same information.

Our agency got a lot of attention in the Philadelphia area, from people interested in local events, news, sports, and memes. In your own region, pizza parlors, sandwich shops, fast food joints, physicians, attorneys, accountants, car companies, car dealers, all want attention.

We feature those business owners by bringing "attention in advance" in the form of video views, likes, responses to Facebook posts, Twitter, and comments, which are DOPAMINE for many local businesses, especially mom-and-pop restaurants. Local newspapers, magazines and mass media outlets don't quite "get it." You get it when you are on a magazine cover, but what fuels this is the ongoing feedback received on a social media platform.

The Big Picture

Drop by a local business (either unannounced, or arrange the visit ahead of time) to record a quick video. Say to the business owner, "We've heard a lot about your business. We'd love to interview you and hear how YOUR business is different." Record a one-minute interview, publish it, get results in advance, then return at a later date to show those results. The next step is to sell consulting or other services.

In contrast: Me-Too Agencies ask for money upfront without building rapport.

It's tempting to simply "make an app" or build something no one is asking for. Look for recurring unresolved issues that appear on your radar, ideally, that relates to an action you're already taking in your business, whether you're a nurse or dealing with local clients.

Getting local clients the "old" way is a nightmare. It involves prospecting, sending letters, emails, marketing to businesses. Those are old-fashioned methods. This way, people ask YOU for help. Build a relationship over time, and more services -- solve MORE problems for this client moving forward.

Don't advertise to your entire country. Cover the local space where you live. Consider a robbery, traffic accident, or a house fire in your local town or city. These events get media attention because they're local. People have a sense of pride in your region, especially when local celebrities and athletes are involved.

Create an audience that is interested in local information. Then, introduce local business to this prospect "list" -- those interested in deals, or at least who want to know what makes local businesses unique. Refer the local physician, attorney, HVAC repairman, or tire servicemen. Other local businesses will recognize the traction and results you deliver. People talk.

"Guess the Final Score" Contest

Scenario: we run a "Guess The Final Score" contest on our "Local Media Asset" Facebook page. In the Philadelphia area, we have a passionate fan base around the Philadelphia Eagles football team during the NFL season.

We state on a Facebook post, "We're giving away a $50 gift card to THIS local restaurant. The first person who correctly guesses the closest final score of this football game wins. The Philadelphia Eagles are playing against the Atlanta Falcons. Tell us who you think will win and what you guess the final score will be. Comment below." Example: Philadelphia Eagles 35, Atlanta Falcons 27. Only one person wins the $50 gift card.

Hundreds of people comment on this "contest" post. Within seconds of commenting, each person gets a Facebook message, via "Messenger bot". That "bot" asks for that person's email addresses to make their entry in the contest "official." The $50 gift card, in this example, is presented by Giovanni Pizza Place. Next, we send an email broadcast to 600 people, who previously opted in when we ran other contests, who have previously been qualified to love contests, pizza, and football -- PLUS they live in the local area.

Another idea: perhaps you're a local dentist. State in a Facebook post: "We love pizza and we know you love pizza. It's important to take care of your teeth. This weekend, we'll promote the upcoming Philadelphia Eagles game, and if you (commenting) guess the correct winning score, we'll send you a $50 gift card to [local pizza place]." This is a great way to network: two businesses work together to further build your "local" list.

Experiment providing different offers. If you wish, offer search engine optimization (Google ranking) and outsource the implementation. Work out some kind of deal, where you refer a local business to a local agency.

Get your foot in the door by providing local companies with excellent results. Local people want news, events, and contests. Business owners want to get in touch with those people. This method of developing relationships turns you into a trusted advisor. You become a connector.

Business Spotlight Video

Let's unpack an easy win for your fledgling agency and Local Media Asset. This only requires an iPhone (or Android device) to record video, and access to social media.

Send this direct message, or email, or telephone call: "Mr. Pizza Shop Owner. This is Drew from Pottstown Local. We love pizza and hear many people love your pizza. We would love to visit and feature your business on our Facebook page. We have thousands of local people interested in learning about your business. Are you available for a one-minute interview?"

There are only two possible answers: yes or no. 95% of the time, the business owner will say, "Yes, when can we do it?" Visit in person, and conduct an interview such as this:

- "Mr. Business Owner, tell us about Dominic's Pizza."
- "We've been serving pizza in the Pottstown area for 25 years."
- "What is your name?"
- "My name is Dominic Zorilli, owner and operator of Dominic's Pizza in Pottstown."

- "What is the most famous item you sell? What's the fan-favorite of Dominic's Pizza?"
- "Our pizza. We serve tomato pie. Many love pepperoni, some people love cheese pizza. We have great personnel and staff."
- "Where can people find you online? Where is your physical location?"
- "DominicsPizza.com. We're located at High Street and Westmoreland."

Broadcast this interview live on Facebook. Advertise, or "boost" the post for $10 to $20, to get thousands of views from viewers in the Pottstown zip code.

After the broadcast is complete, say, "We would love to come back next week to show you the results. Can we meet at [this] time, for five to ten minutes?" Return next week and show 20,000 views on the video. Hundreds of positive comments about that restaurant. Ask the business owner, "Would you like to build a list of people who love your food? You present an offer every single week. Buy one, get one free. Half-off one pizza or stromboli." That business owner can tell you know what you're doing, because you show results.

After building that list of Dominic's Pizza lovers, approach the other 15 local pizzerias. You've already built up an audience for people who love pizza. Show your past results to Giovanni's and Argento's, and ask, "Would you like the same results?" This is the way to differentiate from the Me-Too Agencies. You've already delivered results and built up this Local Media Asset. Facebook, Messenger, and email autoresponders are not expensive platforms.

To recap: Get a local business owner to agree to you filming a quick video. Then ask to return later and show the results! Use those results to convince that business owner to pay you to run contests and ads.

LMA (Local Media Asset)

Build your Facebook page to 2000-5000 local citizens. That's more than enough for you to impress them.

I live in Pottstown, Pennsylvania. My Facebook page is named, "Pottstown Local News and Events." If I approached a local business as "Drew" -- that wouldn't mean much. However, when I'm with "Pottstown Local News and Events" -- the business owner is starstruck at first. YOU have the badge, authority, and credibility.

To recap the video interview that gets your foot in the door: "This is Drew from Pottstown Local. I'm here to interview you about your business." Hold your iPhone steady, or set it up on a tripod. Ask a few basic questions. "What's your name? What's the name of your business? Why did you start this business? Where can people find you online?" Easy softball questions. You don't need to be a mega-interviewer.

Approach these businesses as a "news and events" website. You're not a marketing agency. You're not trying to sell them, only attempting to FEATURE them. Don't overcomplicate it. It becomes easier, and you're less nervous every time. Start simple and small. Invest in yourself and build your asset.

Fringe benefits come from this: press passes, getting behind teams to connect with real events happening in your community. Get to games, go to events. You are the NEW local press.

Your Local Media Asset allows you to compete against multi-million dollar organizations with a simple Facebook page, website, Facebook Messenger list, and email list.

Take action. Level up from the client-chasing merry-go-round. Build a fruitful relationship with local business owners. Solve problems in and around your community. Create a foundation and a platform that you own. Assets that are valuable and sellable.

Drew Griffin from DeliciousMarketing.io can help you grow your business with a "Local Media Asset." Get local clients and a network of businesses in your area to provide services that are easy for you to do and on-demand. Visit LocalWebsiteSystem.com to discover how a Local Media Asset can expand your business and join the private Facebook group at DeliciousMarketing.io/go/group.

Level 4: Team... Let Go of Control & Hire Employees by Lance Tamashiro

Have you heard this saying before? "Don't work IN your business, work ON your business." (Groan!)

What about... "Duplicate yourself so that your business runs on its own?"

Think back to about 10 years ago. Are there one or two SIMPLE pieces of advice you would give your younger self to change your trajectory quite drastically? The problem is, you hear these tired phrases every day, perhaps from mentors or others close to you, but you don't know how to implement that advice.

Those mentors leave out details. At least, they did for me! "They" would say, "Don't work on the day-to-day."

My response: "I would love to sit on the beach, work on my business, and think about the big picture. But I can't do that because I'm putting out fires. If I'm not working IN my business, the money stops."

This applies to you whether you own (or want to own) a brick-and-mortar business, Shopify store, Etsy store, or simply want to sell digital courses.

How do you transition from working in the day-to-day... into becoming the entrepreneur who plans, strategizes, and pushes the buttons? Over the last two years or so, we've worked this out!

It's INEVITABLE That You Will Hire Someone to Work For You

It will happen. However, you may say that's easier said than done. Are you worried you will throw money away, hiring someone to do "stupid" work? Update that Twitter page. Design new business cards. Those activities don't directly make money.

Instead, here's what I propose to you: hire a worker, buy an online course for them, and have THAT course train your worker.

That course could teach how to create something you've always wanted to add to your business. Setup a local "community" website. Create an Etsy store. Build an email affiliate funnel. Decide on your budget, since you'll have to pay your employee, pay for the course, pay for software (or tools), and possibly pay for advertising. Check in with your worker daily to see how they are implementing and if they have questions.

Why Do You Fail (or Struggle) with Outsourcing, In Some Cases, Before You Even Start?

You have so many questions: How much do I pay? How do I manage my employee?

The answer: give up control. It was TOUGH for me to give up control. I thought, "No one else can perform tasks the way I want them done. Nobody can do it better than me, unless I micro-manage."

To make matters worse, you'll fail in outsourcing if you use a "freelance marketplace" like Fiverr or Upwork. Your first transaction, you take a gamble on the person you hire, and it usually goes great. However, you only get good work that FIRST time because the freelancer is looking to get a good rating. Afterwards, the quality from that worker steadily declines.

Solution: Hire a full-time employee who will work for you and take care of your business.

What usually happens when you buy a course? You promise that you'll find time to implement. Perhaps you watch half the videos in that course before moving on to the next course or software.

A "forgotten" course (teaching how to sell shirts and products on Etsy) sat unused on my hard drive for years. I hired an employee with Photoshop skills. I said, "This 15-hour course teaches you how to set it up. Implement this course." We touched-base every day to track progress.

After two weeks, my employee had completed the course, and as a result, setup my Etsy store. I don't even have the password to the account! I told my employee, "Add new products to the store every day. It's your store." One day, he showed me we had 70 sales. The store was making more money than I was paying to that employee!

Assign your employee to learn a course you have not yet watched or implemented. I've only taken action on 5% of the $1000-$2000 courses I've paid for. Are you just as guilty of doing things halfway?

In hindsight, I wish that in previous years, after buying a course, I had hired someone to consume that course, and at the very least, tell me if it was worth implementing.

For example, with the Etsy store, my thought process was, "I've had this course for years. I could find successful stores on Etsy, but is it worth the distraction to dedicate six months?" On the other hand, what about assigning someone to run it every day, until it makes money on its own? People work for us and implement courses. Tasks in our business are completed every day.

Employee Tools: Slack, Loom, Asana

We use free tools to make this happen: a free Slack account to chat with our employees, a free Loom account to record video instructions, and a free Asana account to set recurring tasks, which we check daily.

This is not expensive. It only requires a change in mindset! You already spend the money. Consider how you think nothing of spending $50 to fill up your car's gas tank to get you somewhere! How much do you spend on coffee, bread, bottled water, or ATM fees per year?

Perhaps you've overcome the limiting mindset of spending $1,000 for a course that helps your business grow. There is yet ANOTHER mental obstacle in your way: the cost of implementing. It's somehow easier to spend $1,000 on a course than it is to pay $1,000 for traffic, or $1,000 for your employee to work for many, many hours setting up your course for you.

Be Honest with Yourself!

You will probably only watch half of the course you bought. Even if you watch everything, I doubt you will FULLY implement as you should. Why not go all-in? Tell yourself, "I'll put aside this much money monthly to ensure the course is implemented and continually maintained." If I had adopted this mindset from the beginning -- paid for a course, hired a full-time employee to implement, and stuck with it until it was profitable -- my business would be at least ten times the size as it is now. It would be a HUGE online empire. Buy a course and pay someone to do your homework.

My own ego gets in the way of my progress. I never blindly implemented 100% of any course. I would pick and choose the parts I liked or didn't like. My ego said, "I can set it up better than the course teaches." However, I screwed it up every time.

When I remove myself, tell my employee to watch videos and take action, it is setup the "proper" way. My biggest mistake in business was acting as one single person. Over the course of one year, my "past" self likely bought four $1,000 courses, only putting a fraction of each to use. Instead, I should have spent $1,000 on one course, then $3,000 to pay a full-time employee to work to make it profitable over the next few months.

Considering the worst-case scenario, let's say that after six months of full-time work, the course your employee put into use was NOT effective. Move on. Ask yourself how can you improve in the future.

You probably have a course, sitting and collecting digital dust on your hard drive. You've ALREADY lost money on it because you weren't able to take action on your own.

Assign "bite-sized" tasks (in Asana) that your employee can check off, such as, "Watch Video 1" or "Implement Video 1" or "Spend 1 more hour watching the course."

A very valid concern you may have about hiring your employee: what if that person quits? The system is built. Assign new Asana tasks, and record 3 to 5 minute instructional videos (in Loom) to give their "replacement" daily tasks to keep that website (or store) running every single day.

Hire someone FULL-TIME who works six to eight hours a day. You are completely kidding yourself if you believe that you personally work eight hours a day. Once someone else is checking off the tasks, you'll realize that you are not consistently productive.

Loom, a free browser-based tool, records your screen. Show your employee how to perform a quick, recurring task. Complete some simple action on your computer screen while you narrate your actions, for 3 to 5 minutes. Take the "video sharing" link that Loom gives you, and assign it as a task in "Asana."

The task has a title, description (including your Loom video link), and a due date. Assign that task to one specific person. Send a message on Slack telling your employee to complete that task. If they have trouble finishing, they can message you for help.

Where Do You Find the Money to "Pay" an Employee?

Think about the last four courses you bought and did not implement. How much money could you have now if your Etsy store, Shopify store, or Amazon business was up and running?

Instead of buying four courses, letting your time management and ego get in the way of implementing, buy ONE course. Budget the money you would have spent for the next three courses and hire an employee to build it for you.

Many people who "outsource" or "delegate" fail because they assign boring, managerial, non-profitable activities. Data entry, organizing, accounting. Instead, assign your employee to perform a PROFITABLE task.

Have that employee build SOMETHING for you -- perhaps an Etsy store selling 100 coffee mugs, or an Amazon Kindle account selling 100 e-books. Buy a course that promises a result, or shows a method of making money. Your short-term goal is to make your employee profitable by implementing that course.

You budgeted "seed money" to buy the course, paid your employee hours to learn that course over several hours, and paid them a few more hours to implement. You decided ahead of time that you would allow 3 months, or 6 months, of full-time effort, to make your experiment profitable. Who cares about paying that person monthly, if they are making you money every month?

If you are concerned about trusting your employee at first, use LastPass, a cloud-based password manager. It allows you to share passwords with up to seven people. If you must fire somebody (or they quit, which happens), change the password in one place, then update that set password in LastPass, for those team members who still have access to that particular account and password.

Start your employee slowly until you trust them. This is why it's ideal that you start your employee with a "new" project -- a course you need setup. Grant them access only to that single Amazon account or Etsy store, or WordPress site. That employee only has access to what they need.

As that person works and builds assets for you, they build trust with you, and you give that person access to more "resources."

Our most trusted employee has access to my Facebook ad accounts AND personal Facebook account. He can login, create pages, and place ads, because he earned that trust over time.

Check-ins & Gratitude

We ask every employee to check in (send a message) every morning on Slack, so we know they are present. Each employee begins work at 8:00AM Mountain Time.

Check in with your employees every morning. I put aside time each morning to chat. Near the end of the week, check in with each person individually and ask, "Are you having any problems? Is there anything I can do to make working with me easier? Do you need any resources? Do you not like the way I communicate with you? Do you not like the way I'm doing something? Let me know, because I want a nice working environment for you."

Let them know how much you appreciate and value the work, especially on new or large-scale project.

Build Trust & Scale

Scenario: you bought a course that shows how to use LinkedIn. Give your LinkedIn password to that employee. What if the worst-case scenario happens and this person "steals" your account, somehow? Most sites have "two-factor authentication" which means you can recover access using your phone, if the worst happens.

Another scenario: you setup your WordPress website in a special way so your employee can log into your WordPress site but they can only post content that you must approve. This is called an "editor" account.

Few employers remember to be genuine. Make it a point to say thank you, even if it seems stupid and obvious. Go out of your way to tell someone, "I appreciate you doing this. I like what you do." As you build trust in this relationship, give them access to more accounts as they perform more work for you.

No matter what you think about your online business, you cannot scale without help. If your personal "ceiling" is $2,000, $10,000, or $500,000 a month, you'll wonder why you can't break through.

We've hit ceilings multiple times in our business. We could not scale. You can only put so much mental power into the moving parts of your business. If you want to build a business that scales, remove yourself. Let others take over.

Hiring a profitable employee is addictive. We have many ideas for activities to assign new people we want to hire.

Don't hire an outsourcer from Fiverr or Upwork. Hire an EMPLOYEE. The question isn't, "SHOULD you get an employee?" The question is, "How soon should you hire your SECOND employee?" How soon should you hire your 3rd, 5th, 10th employee? This is how you'll scale. Pay someone to put those "old" courses sitting on your hard drive to use.

Lance Tamashiro would like to help you hire your next employee so you can level up, and get others to do the work for you. Visit TamashiroMarketing.com and schedule an appointment so Lance can find the right fit for you.

Level 5: Networking... Become a Social Podcaster by Robert Plank

Has something in your life involved so much work -- that if, ahead of time, you had KNOWN how much work would be involved, you never would have started?

I've recorded over 725 audio episodes (mostly interviews) for my podcast, MarketerOfTheDay.com, but if I had known in advance that I would record so many, I would have been overwhelmed and never would have started.

Years ago, I heard about a marketing concept from Eben Pagan called "moving the free line." It means: give away your best content for free. For instance, successful business owners and marketers consistently post on social media for free. Matt Mullenweg, creator of WordPress, stated that you could take the "source code" of his software, and make it your own, for free. Elon Musk, creator of the Tesla electric cars, released a pledge stating that he would not initiate any lawsuits against companies using his patents for various batteries and charging devices. Give your best information and intellectual property, away, for free!

In your case, share a recent discovery, or a case study that solved a specific problem. A few tips that could be helpful to someone! "Blog" about it...

The term "blogging" sounds intimidating on its own, but I prefer to think of it like this: create a blog where you can post stories that you cannot profit from AT THIS TIME. If you are a career-minded 9-to-5-er, document something about your profession that is not against company policy and does not reveal trade secrets (or sensitive information). Create a "mini-tutorial" of sorts, and post it publicly.

On the other hand, if you are a self-employed entrepreneur, publish a quick "case study" detailing an experiment -- that either succeeded OR failed -- in your business.

In my blogging journey, I registered my name dot com, RobertPlank.com, and I suggest you do the same. Setup a WordPress blog on that website, and post a video or two. At first, I published one article per month to that blog, but it took me 1-2 days to write each monthly "post." That monthly blog built a list of email opt-in subscribers, but after a few years, I became tired of "scrambling" for a new topic every month.

Podcasting Replaced Blogging

With podcasting, you can click the "record" button, speak out that information you would have otherwise written, and explain it easily, because you spoke it out.

In podcasting, topics you would have blogged about reach an entirely new "non-reader" audience. Some people like to listen to audio in the background during a work-out, while running, or driving.

I blogged monthly for four years, but eventually, I switched to once-per-week podcasting, 15 to 60 minutes per episode. As I approached 100 episodes, I hit a wall. I was bored and wasn't sure if I was repeating myself or getting too detailed.

"Content" is one problem you may have, as a career-climber or entrepreneur. Let's set that problem aside for now, and think about building your network. Socializing, networking, joint venturing... that's not easy for many, and sometimes, is a skill that does NOT come naturally!

Networking & The Interview Model

Have you been in a "networking" situation, at any point during your career or business journey? Have you been stuck in the dreaded "business card exchange" awkward situation?

What happens? You meet someone at some sort of event. You ask the person, "What do you do?" They rattle off some prepared phrase or term, then automatically ask what YOU do. Does anything usually come of such an exchange? Rarely!

When I approach the end of this conversation, I say, "I want to interview you. When we both arrive home, let's set up a time in the coming weeks to meet. I'll ask you questions and record our conversation." At the agreed-upon time and date, I meet in a "Zoom" (online video chat meeting room) to record the quick 20-minute conversation. I ask the person:

- What do you do?
- What is your website address?
- What makes you stand out?

Back to my podcast dilemma: after 100 episodes dishing out ideas, information, discussions, I ran dry on content. I switched to an "interview" model, finding people offline and meeting with them online, asking the above questions, and I was able to break past 100 episodes.

Involve other people in your podcasting, blogging, and marketing. This way, you won't run out of information. You consistently create free material. Be a real marketer and help other people out. In return, they help create content for you. Simultaneously, you introduce yourself and your audience to new experts.

This is an easy, repeatable and predictable way for you to podcast: meet someone for the express purpose of scheduling them as an interviewee on your podcast.

Everyone has difficulties writing in one form or another. However, speaking or explaining things verbally is easier.

How long does a well thought out blog post take? Days? A week, a month? A podcast takes 20 minutes, and it works best if you DON'T waste time preparing for an interview!

Interview an expert for your podcast, and that guest creates your content for free, while making you look like a smart "recommender." No prep is involved in having a conversation. Transform into the interview model to scale.

Advertorial Content

Another "tweak" I would like to suggest when it comes to your teaching, blogging, or podcasting: think not in educational, or advertising terms, but write an "advertorial."

A newspaper article begins by saying, "Breaking News!" New information, but ends with a question, direction, or call-to-action. Perhaps, even with something to buy!

I'm hinting that you need some sort of structure or framework to help you get to the point. Stare at a blank page to write ANYTHING -- a term paper, email, report, blog post -- your mind is blank. You don't know what to write. What words come to mind? Should you "free write" or ramble? That's not interesting. However, if you have a clear focus, you'll know the goal of your "content" -- blog post, video, OR podcast!

The Universal Formula

There's a universal formula to content creation, of ANY form: a book chapter, blog post, or podcast episode. The human brain logically understands information in THIS order:

1. **Why** is this important? What's the problem you're setting up for me?
2. **What** tools will I use to solve this problem? What concepts or PRINCIPLES do I need to know?
3. **How** do I solve this problem?
4. **What-If** this problem is solved, what's the next step for me?

Why, What, How-To, What-If. This helped me SO MUCH when blogging. If wanted to write a blog post about search engine optimization, where would I start?

It's easy to jump into technical terms. Resist that! Sell the PROBLEM first. Why would a casual website visitor care about "search engine optimization?" The person reading that blog post has a website. People need to see it. A prospect searches a phrase in Google. The problem: you, reading this blog post, don't rank in Google. "Why" should YOU care about Search Engine Optimization?

Don't jump into the how-to section. Before I begin to solve this problem, I'll explain what a Google ranking is. What does it mean to be on page one of Google? We know what's in the toolbox. Here are a few simple steps you can use to make this happen.

Beginning any tutorial or content with the "steps" is not accessible. It doesn't help your newbie "beginner" crowd. Establish the problem (WHY), then explain the tools or principles (WHAT), walk through the steps to solve that problem (HOW-TO)... but DON'T stop there!

If you stop after the "how-to" section of your training, you're only dispensing information. People don't know what to do next!

End with the final WHAT-IF section. Provide a call to action: click this link, take this action in your everyday life, leave this blog comment. Don't leave your reader (or listener) hanging!

A very quick recap of the WWHW formula, which is so important for you to understand:

- WHY: why am I here, frustrated, seeking your advice?
- WHAT: what are the principles, concepts, terms, alternatives?
- HOW-TO: a step-by-step solution
- WHAT-IF: what are the next steps or actions?

This applies very well in podcast interviews. I enter the online video chat room at the agreed-upon time and date. I ask, "Are you ready to go?" The answer is yes. I click record, and ask, more or less, the same interview questions every time.

Example: I interview an expert on "meditation" for my Marketer of the Day podcast...

- WHY should listeners use meditation?
- WHAT problem does meditation solve? If people are listening, how do they know if they're listening to the right episode? Even before we jump into what meditation is, what brought you, guest expert, to using meditation as a solution? What's your personal story?
- Next, jump into the "meat" of your content. "Can you tell me about a client you've helped? Can you tell me a story that involves someone who was stuck, and meditation helped solve

some of their problems?" We're throwing out "tips." We're diving into different stories.

- In the end, I recap. There's no harm in you going back by saying, you explained that THIS was the solution to THAT problem.
- To close out the conversation, the question is WHAT-IF... now that people have a few easy problems solved and a taste about what can be done, what is the next step? What website should listeners go to? What OFFER does the guest have ready for listeners? What ACTION is to be taken?

When you meet new people, don't simply exchange my business cards. Schedule a meeting to "get to know each other better." Feature that person as a guest on your podcast. This is how you'll network better.

1-10-100

There are so many possibilities in your podcasting future, but let's stay reasonable so that you can BEGIN reasonably. Ramp up. Start small. Create ONE podcast episode for now. Don't think about ALL the episodes you'll eventually create. Finish that "proof of concept." Prove you can create ONE. Record ONE podcast episode and publish it.

Our course PodcastCrusher.com shows you how to create your podcast. Use your computer's built-in microphone, or your phone to record that FIRST podcast. Here's a prompt to make it easy: talk about yourself, your website, your ORIGIN STORY, and the one thing that makes you stand out. That's your quick "elevator pitch." If you met someone at a live conference or online message board, perhaps a Facebook group, and they asked, "What do you do? How can you help me?" What would be your answer? THAT is your first, five-minute solo podcast episode.

How do you help your clients? Are you a LinkedIn expert? Can you set someone up on social media? Land speaking gigs a for client? How can you help someone else?

The name of my podcast began as "The Robert Plank Show." Name your podcast (at first) as "The [your name] Show." Eventually, after you have PUBLISHED many podcast episodes, graduate from your regular microphone, to a headset, then a studio microphone. Ramp up, just as every successful podcaster, blogger, and business owner, has done.

1-10-100... the "1" symbolizes: get A SINGLE podcast episode published. The "10" in the sequence means this: after you PUBLISH that first episode, brainstorm a handful of topics to fill out episodes 2 through 10, so you don't lose momentum...

What advice made a "mark" on you? What courses have helped you in journey? Do they have affiliate programs? Can you speak out your special link so people can buy that course you recommended? What other marketers (or business owners) can you recommend?

You probably have, within you, right now, at LEAST 10 helpful stories that can help others. With a little meditation, you could recall ten stories that illustrate how you've struggled. Perhaps they illuminate problems you've solved or things that have changed your life. Conjure up these ten "topics"... and then use the WWHW template (Why, What, How-To, What-If) to FLESH OUT the sub-topics (talking points) within your podcast episode...

WWHW: The Universal Formula

Example: you want to record a podcast episode explaining how to setup a YouTube presence. Your podcast episode content: WHY would I want to use YouTube? WHAT YouTube (and video) terms do I need to know? HOW do set myself up on YouTube? WHAT-IF I'm setup on YouTube? What's the next step?

This is the universal formula. Record "an" episode to set yourself up on a podcast, then consider ten fun topics... but make the ultimate goal (knowing the details are not fully formed yet)... 100 episodes.

When I created my podcast, I promised myself to ONLY publish 100 episodes. At episode 50, I planned to announce that "The Robert Plank Show" (podcast) would end, as an attention-getter. People would say, "Please, keep the podcast going." As I approached episode 80, 90, 95, I had planned to end the show.

How many TV shows lasted too long (Seinfeld, How I Met Your Mother, Heroes) versus TV shows that

ENDED with people wanting more (Breaking Bad, Mad Men, The Shield)?

Back to the "interview concept." Contact your BEST customers over the years. Do you have an email list? Facebook following? Which of your customers or your clients are gutsy enough to hop on a phone call with you?

What about your mentors? Idols? People you've bought from? People you look up to?

Different podcast interviews have different results. Take action. Don't let the technical details stop you. Focus on the people you'll contact, and less on the equipment.

When interviewing your guest, play "devil's advocate." Get into a newbie mindset. For example, when interviewing someone about mindfulness meditation, I might ask, "What would you say to someone who thinks meditation doesn't work?" Interview someone about podcasting. Ask, "I'm sure I have to buy a lot of expensive equipment in order to podcast. Is that right?"

Listeners are thinking about "the elephant in the room" that isn't being asked. Give any advice to your audience, in podcasting or any other form. Your "listener" is listening to your words, while already talking themselves out of taking any action. The person is afraid, overwhelmed and confused. Play devil's advocate to blow past sensitive issues and keep the conversation moving.

Monetization

Podcast "gurus" tell you to get a "sponsor" for your podcast. Listen to most podcasts and you'll discover that most of them promote "affiliate programs." They make a commission from every sale. Audible, Squarespace, ClickFunnels. The way to make money on your podcast is to send people to OFFERS -- your product, or affiliate links (recommendations) of bigger brands.

My favorite technique to get attention on my podcast: add an email signature link on the bottom of "broadcast" emails. The very bottom is a link (changing every few days) pointing people to the latest podcast episode. Here's an email message, buy this offer if you want it, P.S., at the bottom, listen to the latest podcast episode.

Google search "podcast directories." There are hundreds of places where you can submit your podcast "feed" -- the special link search engines (like Google) use to find your latest podcast episode.

Traffic from Interviewees

More low hanging fruit: interview someone on your podcast, and days or weeks later, email that person, saying, "Our episode is live. Here's the link. Promote this to your audience."

Scenario: I attend the Lance Tamashiro Show as a guest for one episode, promoting Podcast Crusher. When the episode goes live, I'll send the link to my list and post it on Facebook. Use your podcast guest, not just for content, but for traffic, even AFTER the episode goes live!

Consider ANY platform where you have ANY sort of traffic -- Facebook, YouTube, podcasting, LinkedIn -- mention your OTHER platforms to get people paying attention and listening to you. Post a YouTube video, and mention your podcast! On your podcast, mention your Facebook page! Post a link to your latest podcast episode ON your Facebook page. Send your email list to your latest YouTube video. Get the point?

The "WWHW" structure and mindset is crucial. Why, What, How-To, What-If. This applies to podcast interviews, content creation, blogging, videos, webinars, presentations, personal relationships, and business building.

Pick up on what people SAY. Move the conversation forward. Unpack ideas. Be aware of which conversation "stage" you live in at the present moment: WHY (context of the problem), WHAT (tools in the toolbox you'll use), HOW-TO (steps to solve the problem), and WHAT-IF (next steps to take in a larger sense).

Get into the mindset of "helping others." Rely on the WWHW (Why, What, How-To, What-If) template at first. This reduces the initial anxiety and awkwardness of taking action. In a podcast interview, I start with the why, the what, go to the how-to, and close with what-if.

The interview, conversation, problem-solving "sequence" becomes subconscious and automatic for you. You'll use it again and again, I promise!

Robert Plank is a podcaster (<u>MarketerOfTheDay.com</u>) *who wants to show you how to use the WWHW formula (Why, What, How-To, What-If) to level up and finally stop struggling in your life and business. Get his book at* <u>WWHWBook.com</u> *and his podcasting course at* <u>PodcastCrusher.com</u>.

Level 6: Achievement... Find Your Goals & Hidden Money by Syndee Hendricks

What are you lacking? Do you have a loved one that you want to take care of? Do you want to take a vacation with someone you love? Do you want to live in your dream home and drive an amazing car? Do you need to expand your business? You need money for all these goals!

Las Vegas. I was speaking at a conference, and Thomas Hydes approached me during a break to hire me as his business coach and consultant. He revealed that he was a classically trained opera singer. My first response was to blurt out that I didn't sing, read music, or play an instrument, so I didn't know how to help him!

Rather than walk away, I listened to his story. Thomas wanted me to help him with his speaking and coaching business, which I could do! It brought back some bad memories. I was rejected from seventh grade choir and still had scars!

Had I written him off, I would have lost a great client, fabulous radio show co-host, awesome course-creation business partner, corporate international co-trainer. Imagine how much success and LEVELING UP that could have been lost had we not worked together!

We both would have lost out HUGELY if I had not taken on this talented person -- client -- turned business partner! We became great friends.

Perspective

The problem of how to earn more money for the things needed not only to survive, but to have a great life! If you live in the United States, you can number yourself amongst the top six percent of the richest people in the world. If you have the opportunity to experience living under a roof with clean, safe drinking water you can consider yourself lucky compared to most of the rest of the world. Spending time reflecting on your personal gratitude to create happiness is a time proven tool and on how lucky you are for the many gifts that you've already received is extraordinarily valuable.

Gaining perspective of those wonderful things you have in your life can give you a real feeling of satisfaction that can transform your life.

When I hear the family stories of American immigrants that came to the United States with just a few dollars, and in the course of one lifetime, evolved into a successful family -- I hear, see, and feel gratitude in their storytelling of the question posed of how to earn the money for the things needed for a great life!

In the minds of those first generation immigrants in the United States, there existed an idea: the idea of something better and the courage to move to a new country was fueled by another powerful emotion -- desire. Desire is that magical fuel that has changed the course of human history.

Desire has caused the landscape of the world to change. In just the last 100 years the world has found itself built up with giant concrete and steel skyscrapers, massive roads, state-of-the-art bridges, tunnels through mountains, and cities creating homes for double-digit millions of people. Desire is the fuel that has created everything that you see.

While that creates everything you see including the device you're reading this on (or the book you're holding), MONEY is the medium by which it is achieved. The wages paid to workers to build skyscrapers or automobiles, the wages paid to engineers to design bridges, and the wages paid to salesmen to sell software give medium to turn ideas fueled by desire into our amazing reality.

This is why you need more money. The ideas that you desire to turn into reality require money.

How Can I Profit From It?

Recently, I spoke to an extraordinarily financially successful gentleman -- by any standard! He shared an adage he learned early in life:

- When presented with a financial obstacle, a poor person says, "I can't afford it."
- A middle class person says, "I can find a way to afford it."
- A rich person asks, "How can I PROFIT from it?"

For example, when faced with the possibility of a pricey cab ride, two wealthy entrepreneurs invented Uber as a solution. They examined a problem and asked the question, "How can I make money from this?" Then created a solution. Years ago I played a game at a business class hosted by Marshall Thurber. The game was like any other game you would encounter, with one great exception: there was a bank. I was stumped. Why was there a bank in the game?

A wealthy gentleman won the game because he knew how to use the bank as leverage to win that game. Utilizing the bank to finance the playing of the game was the key to victory. Most of us didn't realize that the keys to winning the game were to use the bank. **It was a wonderful metaphor for life because one of the keys to winning a business game is finance.**

In order to turn your idea into reality you need to find money. You need more money than you currently have. There are many avenues for getting more money, including grants, loans, sales, wages, trades, bartering, creative financing tactics, begging, borrowing and stealing. Tony Robbins says, "There is no such thing as a lack of resources, only a lack of RESOURCEFULNESS."

Hidden Money

The greatest way for you to find money for your business and for the things that you desire is for you to find hidden money.

What is hidden money? It is the collection of skills and tools that you personally possess that will help you create more money to fuel the ideas that you desire to turn into reality. What if you had a detailed path to find your hidden money? What if you had a team of experienced people to support your journey to finding your hidden money? How would you feel if you had a program that guided you through tried-and-true information, templates, and coaching that supported your finding hidden money?

There are only 24 hours in the day for every single person, you also need ways to manage your time and need a simple way -- a way that's effective for you, a way that gives you the time that you need in order to achieve the goals that are important to you that are part of your greatest desires.

Mindset is extraordinarily important. It is your vehicle for creating your goals, and staying on the path to achieving them whether you are confronted with obstacles that are real or imagined. A book once stated that "The Obstacle Is The Way." Often, the obstacle is the PATHWAY. Many times, I have overcome the obstacles to achieving my goals by having a coach, and a program, to support the discovery in overcoming these obstacles.

It is the combination of skills, talents, and resources that either you possess or you get support to learn that gives you the power to create money that you didn't know existed. Let's talk about some of the ways that people find hidden money.

Firstly, there is **goal setting**. The first step is to figure out what's really important to you. Sift through your ideas. Select the best one! Create a worthwhile goal that you truly desire. There many different ways you can set goals:

- Write the goals in a manner that is measurable, clear, concise, and has a completion date. Have a clear idea of your "why."

- An action plan gives assurance that you have a plan to achieve your goal(s).

- Discover a way to scale obstacles realized along the way.

- Find a coach (that resonates with you) who can hold you accountable, and help you overcome obstacles.

Secondly, there are personal skills, ways of being, and ideas that largely contribute to the success of finding your hidden money.

- Self-Esteem, Self-Confidence, What you really want, Mission Statement

- Mindset, Values, Energy

- Visualization, Affirmations of what is important and what you really want

And thirdly, there is Time Management, or as we call it: Find Your Inner CEO, which supports well beyond time management!

- Find a program that instructs you in ways that you can maintain that shows you where your time goes, and a way to plan your time.

- Find the discipline to keep the program up every day

- Create your to do lists based on your goal-setting action plan

- Find a consultant or a coach that resonates with you to help with the obstacles and holds you accountable.

- Find online support that helps keep it all straight!

Your Self-Esteem and Self-Confidence are most important, as they are your drivers. Examples are below of famous people who let those two things affect them, and overcame to live lives as superstars!

Celebrities, Politicians, Authors, and Inventors who struggled with Low Self-Esteem:

- Lady Gaga, Joan Rivers, Jennifer Lopez, Arnold Schwarzenegger, Larry King, Selena Gomez...

- Demi Lovato, Chris Pratt, Serena Williams, Kate Winslet, Hellen Keller...

- Thomas Edison, Theodore Roosevelt, Albert Einstein, Ralph Waldo Emerson, Abraham Lincoln...

What if they had not been able to overcome the obstacle of low self-esteem or own their self-confidence? Very important things in our world as we know it today would be changed!

What if YOU don't overcome your obstacles that are keeping you from up-leveling and finding your hidden money? Sometimes we all need a trained mind or a second set of eyes to look at what we are doing and see our blind spots!

A client recently told me this: "I was struggling to get to my next level. I had a coaching session with Syndee ...and became really clear on my action steps. I had my first MILLION DOLLAR sales month and biggest commission check ever!"

Syndee Hendricks and Thomas Hydes, online course creators and best-selling authors, are corporate real world trainers, online trainers, and radio hosts. Syndee is a certified business consultant, intuitive coach, speaker, and twelve-time author. Thomas is a certified world-class speaker and coach, voice trainer, classically trained opera singer, and three-time author. Tune in to the "Imagine More Success Radio Show" at ImagineMoreSuccess.net. *Then, visit* FindHiddenMoney.com *and sign up for FREE 26 Business Tips delivered to your inbox every week!*

Level 7: Health & Wellness... Get to the Root Cause of Your Weight Issues by Tammy Wasinger

"I've tried every popular diet out there and I still cannot lose the weight that I need to or keep it off!" Lauri cried. Over the last 10 years, 20 pounds crept up on her. She was a middle-aged corporate executive mother of two, and sought me for help.

She explained her dilemma: "You name it: Weight Watchers, keto, Paleo. I've joined gyms, tried intermittent fasting, starving myself for days. I'd lose a few pounds, but the minute I began a normal healthy diet, the pounds returned, sometimes more than I lost! I'm at my wit's end and don't know what to do."

She could have approached her family physician for a sleeping pill to help her sleep. Perhaps, an antidepressant, since she was feeling down about not being able to lose weight. Instead, Lauri explored Functional Medicine Wellness Advocates. She wanted us to get to the root cause of her ailments.

Upon further inquiring, I discovered Lauri was experiencing low energy. She had trouble staying or falling asleep. She awoke around 2:30AM most nights, often emotional or irritable. She was foggy and had trouble concentrating, had intense cravings for sweet (and salty) foods, with an afternoon slump every day. Low energy (and fatigue from lack of sleep) affected her performance at work. She became more absent-minded with age. For example, she would forget why she came into a room. Lauri just wasn't as sharp as she used to be.

Could this be YOUR story? Let's say you saw yourself with some (or all) of these symptoms: trouble losing the weight, and keeping it off -- or experiencing added symptoms such as Lauri's as you age. The cause may surprise you...

Conventional logic states that calories in/calories out is THE way to lose weight. Expend more calories than you take in, automatically lose the pounds. However, hundreds of people still struggle with weight loss after trying this method. Obesity is at an all-time high. If "calorie restriction" was the solution, why do so many people still search for a solution? Weight loss can be much more complex than eating less and expecting to lose the weight. Research has found that your gut bacteria can play a large role in what you crave, how your body uses stored fat, and how you gain or lose weight.

They Lied to You!

In the late 1970's, the government told us fat was bad. It was the primary cause of poor health and weight gain. Americans eliminated fat from their diet. Food producers came to the rescue! Low-fat and fat-free products appeared on grocery store shelves. Health conscious dieters ate eggs without yolks and consumed fat-free crackers, cookies and candies. Remember Snackwell's Devil's Food Cake Fat Free Cookies?

If food manufacturers reduce fat, they must replace that with something else. That "something else?" Grains, sugar, sugar substitutes. We were taught that as long as we reduce the amount of fat, eating plenty of carbs and sugar were fine. The consequence? The largest obesity crisis we've ever seen! Americans gained more weight during this fat-free era than any other time in history!

Obesity rates prior to the 1980's was 12-14%. After the change in diet from the 80's to fat-free, obesity levels shot up to 22-25% in one decade. As of 2018, nearly

40% of all adults over the age of 20 in the U.S – about 93.3 million people – are obese, according to data published in JAMA in 2018. Wow!

Another huge change in our Standard American Diet (SAD)... the introduction of High Fructose Corn Syrup (HFCS). It was a cheap alternative and made foods taste sweeter, an instant hit. Many foods and beverages replace sugar with HFCS. It's astounding how much sugar, in any form, Americans eat per year. Two hundred years ago, the average American ate two pounds of sugar a year. In 1970, we ate 123 pounds of sugar per year. Today, the average American consumes almost 152 pounds of sugar in one year. This is 3 pounds (6 cups) of sugar consumed in a week!

Sugar (especially in HFCS form) is NOT safe to consume, but I will save that for another day. It alters the "microbiome" of your gut. The microbiome is the genetic material of all microbes -- bacteria, fungi, protozoa, and viruses -- that live inside the human body. Trillions live in your body. They outnumber human cells 10-to-1. You are only 10% human and 90% microbial!

Pesticides Are Not Meant for Human Consumption

Do fat-free foods, high grains, sugar intake, and modified high fructose corn syrup sound scary enough? There's a new problem affecting today's food supply: consuming unhealthy Genetically Modified Organisms (GMOs). A GMO is an organism whose DNA is altered or modified in some way through genetic engineering. The food industry and government have claimed these foods are safe. However, "Genetically modified foods have been linked to toxic and allergic reactions, sickness, sterile and dead livestock, and damage to virtually every organ studied in lab animals," according to the Institute for Responsible Technology.

According to the Non-GMO Project, "Most developed nations do not consider GMOs to be safe. 60+ countries, including Australia, Japan and the European Union, have significant restrictions or bans on the production and sale of GMOs."

As You Sow is a nonprofit environmental watchdog focusing its research on how corporate actions affect our environment, including food production. According to Christy Spees, a program manager with

As You Sow, GMO foods are dangerous "because the modifications are centered around resistance to toxic substances, such as pesticides and certain fertilizers. When dangerous chemicals are applied, plants use them to grow, and the food itself can be detrimental to our health."

In 2015, 93% of corn, 94% of soybeans, and 94% of cotton produced in the US were genetically modified strains. Most of that ends up as animal feed, ethanol, or corn syrup. Many GMO crops are genetically engineered to be Roundup-tolerant. Roundup is a common weed killer used by farmers and homeowners. Roundup is the brand name for the herbicide: glyphosate.

In studies, glyphosate herbicides were applied to growing plants. The produced plant material was not analyzed for glyphosate residues. Independent research found glyphosate-tolerant plants accumulate glyphosate residues at unexpectedly high levels. The residues? Passed onto consumers!

Scientific literature and regulatory conclusions regarding glyphosate and glyphosate-based herbicides show a mix of findings, making the safety of the herbicide a hotly debated subject: In 2015, the World Health Organization's International Agency for

Research on Cancer (IARC) classified glyphosate as "probably carcinogenic to humans" after reviewing years of published and peer-reviewed scientific studies. The team of international scientists found there was a particular association between glyphosate and non-Hodgkin's lymphoma.

In 2018, a jury ruled in favor of Dewayne "Lee" Johnson, the terminally ill former school groundskeeper who became the first person to take Monsanto to trial over Roundup. The judge stated that Monsanto "acted with malice" and knew or should have known its chemical was dangerous and failed to warn consumers about the risks. Johnson was awarded $289 million.

In March 2019, a federal court civil jury awarded another man $80 million for his claim that Roundup was a substantial factor in causing his non-Hodgkin's lymphoma.

In May 2019, a jury awarded a couple $2 billion in punitive damages after concluding that sustained exposure to Roundup led to their cancer diagnoses. They also had non-Hodgkin's lymphoma.

Hopefully, the tide will change regarding the food industry. In the meantime, be aware of the food choices you make. Eating these harmful foods negatively alter the gut microbiome and ultimately may lead to cancer, and other serious diseases.

Healing Begins

Lauri tried "everything" yet failed to lose weight and didn't know why. She had a negatively altered microbiome. Her good and bad bacteria were out of balance. This might sound simple, but can cause serious problems. She tested at toxic levels for Glyphosate poisoning.

Her altered microbiome caused her body to stop some beneficial enzymes and other functions that would fully eliminate toxins and other harmful organisms. Her liver and other organs did not function properly. She was not absorbing the nutrients, vitamins, minerals and amino acids she needed to aid in normal eliminations of harmful chemicals and toxins. Instead, she absorbed them in her fat cells!

This affected her estrogen and other hormone levels that directly affected weight loss and caused malfunctions to her detox pathways. This kept her body in a toxic state and prevented her from easily losing weight.

We created a personalized meal plan, making changes to her diet. Lauri also eliminated a few bad habits, for example, drinking 3-4 diet colas per day, and eating too much sugar. She reinoculated her gut with the right probiotic she needed and added supplements that helped eliminate the buildup of toxins and aided in detoxing her overtaxed organs.

We recommended lymphatic drainage techniques and a few other physical detox strategies to help her body eliminate the build up of toxins.

Within a month, she noticed improvements: more energy to exercise and plan healthy meals on her own for the week. She was unable to do this before beginning this protocol with such low energy. Her mind cleared and the afternoon fogginess was gone. She responded to a few changes and additions. Her body began to heal. In a few months, she lost 20 pounds.

What Can You Do To Improve Your Health?

Can you relate to some or all of Lauri's ailments? What you can do to lose weight? Maybe you don't feel good, or you lack the energy you SHOULD have for some reason. Find a functional medicine wellness coach or physician. They are critical in helping you discover the root cause of your ailment. Your issue may not be the same altered bacteria Lauri struggled with. A good practitioner that can search for these is the only way to find out.

Eliminating bad habits is a good next step. Replace diet or high sugar drinks with water (or healthy tea) to stop damaging your gut. Drink at least half your body weight in filtered water. Many chemicals in sodas and sugary drinks are found to cause cancer.

Reflect on what you normally eat for meals and snacks. How many of your meals are laden with sugars, refined grains and trans fats? Lauri ate out at least once per day, ingesting high-carb and high-fat (most likely trans-fat) meals.

Occasional indulging of a Big Mac and fries is not a problem, but understand that your body must literally "detox" non-nourishing food. Anything more than an occasional treat adds up. It hurts your body and accelerates aging. It alters the good and bad gut bacteria. As you saw with Lauri, that can cause further problems that have a domino effect on your health.

Sleep is another critically important element. Many people do not get enough, and feel that they're LAZY if they get too much sleep. They underestimate the importance of sleep's healing aspects. Some lack quality rest because of their out-of-balance bodies. Getting into a healthier state of being will help you sleep more deeply and restfully. Lauri had issues with falling back to sleep when she woke up around 2am. Healing her gut helped heal her cortisol and hormone issues. She could stay asleep or fall back readily if awakened.

Food is the best place for body nourishment, however, sometimes, you must add a few supplements. Nutritional quality of food is declining. Modern intensive agricultural methods have depleted essential minerals from the soil, impacting food grown in them.

Potatoes have 30% less magnesium, 35% less calcium, 45% less iron and 47% less copper than they once did.

Carrots have 75% less magnesium, 48% less calcium, 46% less iron and 75% less copper.

In addition, if you do not consume the proper amount of vitamins, minerals, and amino acids your body needs, you will most likely have altered good and bad bacteria, which could eventually harm other areas of your body. Supplements replenish what is lacking.

If weight loss was only about calories in/calories out, it would be easy to cut out a few bad habits and lose weight. Multiple factors affect weight loss. Healing the gut is the primary way to reach that objective.

Tammy Wasinger is the Founder of Root Awakenings, a
Licensed Practical Nurse for 30 years, and a Functional
Medicine Health Coach. Tammy is also Board Certified by
the American Association of Drugless Practitioners and a
Member of the National Association of Nutrition
Professionals. Schedule your complimentary Root
Awakening Session at:

Discover.YourRootAwakenings.com

Level 8: Home... Make Your Living Space Work for You by Jeanette Chasworth

What clothing items sit in your closet at this very moment? Can you honestly declare that EVERY item fits like a glove? Does EVERY item authentically capture who you are today? I doubt it!

Some of your clothes come from a bygone era from your younger days. Example: when I was a high school sophomore, I bought an adorable outfit in London. I'll never wear it again, but I can't bring myself to part with it because of the associated happy memories.

Some clothes were trendy for their original era but look silly in the 21st century. Perhaps a sale was too hard to resist. They weren't the perfect fit but represented an "ideal" size. If you only hit the gym and lost a few pounds, it would fit!

At some point, you have worn a "lucky" outfit to interviews, dates, days you wanted to feel "on top of the world." Even after they have become threadbare, letting go would court cosmic disaster.

What about all those jackets, shoes, and hats you forgot about? These items didn't clutter up your closet all at once, did they? You never noticed, but your closet became overstuffed. There was no more room for hangers to accommodate any new purchases to better define your current sense of self, style, and voice.

Such is the pattern that unfolds in your entire living space. The cumulative clutter represents a timeline of where you've been and where you are now. You're reluctant to part with anything nostalgic, and there's no reason you have to! However, too frequently, you succumb to the belief that you must build your dwelling around a past that is no longer relevant.

Who Are You and Where Do You Want to Be?

I awoke one day and decided I didn't like my house. I wasn't sure what riled my senses and made me depressed. In desperation, I grabbed my keys and walked around the block. When I returned, I rang my doorbell, waited a few minutes, then entered the house as if it belonged to a client, and I was seeing it for the first time. A proverbial lightbulb came on!

With a designer's eye, I stepped into the living room and took stock of the conflicting "noise" competing for my attention. This was the house of a woman who had dealt with the death of her father, estrangement of her family, fracturing of friendships, and a long marriage with a painful end. Ghosts shouted from every corner in the colors, textures, furnishings, and décor my earlier self had once enthusiastically embraced.

And yet, I saw no presence of the strong, focused, independent woman I had rediscovered.

Reinvent, Recreate, Reimagine

Back to the closet analogy: hanging something on a rack or (placing it on a shelf) does NOT mean you are stuck with that item forever. You are constantly subjected to change and disruption in your life. Love, loss, illness, employment, relocation. Your home is the last "instrument" you consider to heal and grow. Your home wasn't cluttered overnight. Maintaining the status quo is (supposedly) easier and less stressful than taking bold steps to reinvent, recreate and reimagine a happier, positive outcome. The more stagnant you allow your living space to become, the less growth you'll experience as a being.

Splashing a new coat of paint or swapping out window treatments will not solve your problem. My approach: **fully embrace the healing and therapeutic aspects of design.**

Some of my clients emerge into "the world" of singlehood as a product of death or divorce. Some have lost their parents and feel like adult orphans. Everything in their space is a testament to an "us" that no longer exists. Understandably, they are reluctant to put their "oneness" into the spotlight. One client in particular was keeping unfashionable clothes that no longer fit, in a subliminal hope that "perhaps" keeping everything as it once was would somehow revive past loved ones. Trust me, it won't.

Make Room!

Make room in YOUR closet for new items, experiences, and perspectives. This is the gateway to liberating your empowerment. Moving an outdated item from the past, into a less prominent location (i.e. off the "shrine" of the fireplace mantle) does NOT diminish the fondness of that memory. Instead, it encourages an honest assessment of what's truly important in the here and now.

Your first step to moving forward: walk around the block. Walk in through your front door to see your home through the eyes of someone who doesn't know you.

If you're ready for that journey of self-discovery, I'd like to take it with you. After working with me, the typical client describes their new space as "a visual expression of their personality." Their home no longer feels chaotic. It's become a sanctuary! Colors and textures create a sense of peace and comfort. That client's energy harmonizes with their home. My portfolio illustrates great diversity in design, as my philosophy is unbounded by a particular style. My inspiration draws from the desires that your house "whispers in my ear."

Jeanette Chasworth, The Color Whisperer, is the author of, "What's Color Got To Do With It." She creates incredible rooms and homes. When starting a new project, she listens to YOUR needs and desires, utilizing intuition and design knowledge to create a unique environment that weaves together your tastes, preferences, and functional needs to create a space that reflects your personality.

- Website: TheColorWhisperer.com
- Phone: 626-485-6354

Level 9: Inner Wisdom... Communicate Clearly by Melinda Kelly

You are a resourceful person. When you were younger, you asked question after question, but adults "shushed" you. In high school, someone called you "dumb." One day, at your first job, someone asked, "Do you even know what you're doing?"

It's tough to search for answers on your own because some situations have no handbook. Your greatest success is saying, "I need help. Who can help me?"

Get a Coach

You wouldn't think twice about hiring a life teacher, manager, sports trainer, tennis instructor, or golf coach. But hiring someone to coach you in life or business is difficult and personal!

Don't be afraid to ask for help. Consult a friend or family member who was successful in business or the area you need help. You could be happier, live life with less difficulty, and be more financially successful if you weren't "slogging through" so much.

An important question to ask yourself: "What is the quality of my life?"

When asking for advice, someone who KNOWS you has biased perceptions of you. However, an objective person who doesn't "know" you is a good thing. When you deal with an independent third party, there's no history to get in the way. That person listens to your hopes and dreams.

We also put a range of roles into it when we deal with somebody we know very well. You need sensible advice in today's realities.

Third Party Advice

Get the best advice from an independent third party who doesn't know your past. Ask people who they would recommend. See how you fit with them in terms of values, and if you resonate with one another. But it's more than just seeing if you like each other, it's knowing who you are. You have traits and tendencies. You don't realize the daily habits that sabotage you.

Have you been in a meeting where someone was talking and you thought to yourself, "I know that!" You were busy being pre-occupied with your existing knowledge. The presenter dropped a pearl of wisdom. You missed it, because you were busy thinking about yourself. You think you know everything and don't realize there are a few things you don't know.

Don't Ignore That Sign

I keep coming across the saying, "I've HEARD of that so I don't need to LISTEN." I wasn't aware of this within myself until I saw others with this same self-sabotaging behavior.

If you keep coming across the same advice and not implementing, that's a sign.

> *"Your friends admire you for your qualities, but*
> *they love you for your flaws."*
> *-- Unknown*

Long ago, I decided I would take a brave adventure. I signed up with a writing coach, attended the first meeting, did the assignment, came back, presented, and was savaged. I took notes and thought, "I'm learning." I redid the assignment, brought it back and was savaged AGAIN. It chilled and scared me from working with anyone again. Growth can be painful!

A friend recommended a different writing coach. I felt like a gypsy, moving from person to person. In your case, perhaps a coach or mentor brought you from Point A to Point B. They outlived their usefulness (in one way or another), and a new coach brought you to Point C, and someone else, to Point D, of leveling up, and so on. Why wouldn't YOU continue this arc?

The next coach in my journey was also excellent. I signed up for her program, and halfway through, I realized that I had not been paying attention. I was not ready for what she was presenting.

I had been arrogant! It wasn't her but ME who was not ready for growth. It was hard to acknowledge my mistake but it helped me have a stronger, healthier relationship with those I worked with.

In your journey, you experienced painful growths, evolving from one mentor to another, seeking help to get where you needed to go. Personally, I find that challenging, similar to breaking-up or parting ways. I am specific when I seek coaching. Last year, I worked with my speaking and got the help I needed to progress. At times, I SABOTAGED my learning. I incorrectly thought that program outlived its usefulness. I wondered if I let that coach, or myself, down.

Authority Figures

Examine your relationship with authority figures, because you don't always realize what your relationship with these mentors and coaches, is if you don't look at what you do with authority figures. Trade your resources for their knowledge. Both coach and student (you) mutually benefit from the experience. Everything should be mutually advantageous.

I still maintain relationships with past coaches. Despite my challenges, I value her approach to things that she does that I still find value in.

I dug deep into my purpose in each relationship. I've had to live with these truths I've discovered. It's made me reassess each coaching relationship along with seeing what they have legitimately offered and given, even the issues and problems I encountered.

Some coaches say, "Here's my course, this is what I do, good luck, and if you need a refresher or additional training, come back and we'll talk." It depends on your dynamic.

Socratic Method

If there's friction, or some other conflict, the "Socratic Method" helps. I love asking questions. Often, you know the answers, but you need someone to help direct you. One client had recently retired. She was drafting crazy plans. I pointed out this was a move based upon a child that hadn't been born to her daughter who hadn't gotten married, on the belief that they might eventually move to that city. The irony: everybody ended up in the city SHE had moved to.

She's now looking at what to do with all this free time in a new city. I helped her go through places where she can showcase her talents and find funding. It was a lovely experience working together to find the best use of time and talents. She's looking into teaching at an adult college and we created a course program. She's excited about the possibilities. Her hopes and dreams were way ahead of the curve.

There Is No Guarantee

In our lives, we create our map. No baby would be born if we had to wait for guarantees. No one would get married if it was absolute. Life is a beautiful adventure that gets us giddy every so often. My mom said she wished she could wrap us in a protective bubble before bringing us to this planet. That's everybody's dream, but it's not a practical way to live life.

Half the fun is when you get lost on a road, discover a thousand-mile ball of twine and laugh about it forever. Many of the great moments of life are when we least expect them.

> *"Success is getting what you want.*
> *Happiness is wanting what you get."*
> *-- Dale Carnegie*

Too often, you chase someone else's dream and take the easy route. Instead of understanding your values and priorities, you follow someone else's vision.

There are several ways to succeed. But do you have complete success if you're not happy? My biggest wish is that you know yourself enough to know what will fulfill you, which will bring you happiness and success.

In this digital age, it's easy to fall into the "Facebook envy" trap observing the seemingly perfect lives of others. Their lives might not be as happy as you think! You getting everything you ever wanted might not be the blessing you think it is.

Don't chase someone else's dream. Be happy. Work hard on what fulfills you. Your path most likely contains tiny bumps, full turnarounds, and bombs blowing up in front of you. That's no fun, but you get up, keep going and continue that journey.

*Melinda Kelly from <u>MelindaJKelly.com</u> is the author of
"Finding Your Coach: Diving Deep Within." Visit her
website to go to discover what you need to know to find
your coach and stop resisting.*

Level 10: Confidence... Your Journey to Well-BEing by Colleen Rekers

What did you want to be when you grow up? A child's answer: a ballerina, astronaut, police officer, fashion designer. Rockstar! President!

Children are creative, big dreamers. Their ideas of what they can accomplish are LIMITLESS. They become part of every fairy tale they read. ANYTHING is within reach.

As you've aged, your answers to this question have changed. I'm guessing that your career choice is far from what you once dreamed. Opportunities have led you down different roads. Perhaps you gave up on your dream or lost sight of what you wanted from life.

Years later, is something missing? Can you relate to the feeling of being unfulfilled, bored, uneasy? What do you do with this uncomfortable feeling? Accept it as part of normal life?

Where Did Your Dreams Go?

What happened to your belief that you could be anything you wanted to be, and more?

You could claim that children don't know what they don't know. Perhaps their plans are playful fantasies! However, children have the right idea: dream big and believe in yourself. You can BE anything and DO anything.

> *"Someday you will be old enough to start reading fairy tales again."*
> -- C.S. Lewis

It's never too late to dream again. Re-write your next chapter, no matter how your story began.

From the day you were born, you were influenced by your surroundings. Family, community, school. Every word, gesture, vibration, experience. These factors impacted the person you became, mentally and physically. Regardless of your good (or bad) upbringing, every experience has impacted your belief system -- how you think and act.

Beliefs & Limitations

Until age 11, I spent most of my time with my grandmother and aunt. This dynamic impacted me. I didn't grow up with siblings, which influenced my desire for a large family. Dedication, work ethic, kindness, love, and compassion came from those people surrounding me during adolescence. My baggage also included a demand of high expectations which lead to a fear of failure. Anxiety, depression, poor nutrition, struggle with weight management, lack of confidence, addiction, and thoughts of scarcity.

When you identify those beliefs (often subconscious, never identified or challenged) that have always surrounded you, you will understand the origins of those self-imposed limitations.

Have you thought, "I can't do that?" At times, your mind created excuses, keeping you trapped inside your comfort zone. The truth is that you are limitless, but the thoughts that limit your beliefs prevent you from dreaming and growing. This keeps you stuck, unfulfilled, bored, and unsatisfied. It prevents you from living your best life.

When my five children were still in diapers, I lost my husband to addiction, and became a single mom. I thought my life was over. Many nights, after putting the children to bed, I closed the door to my room, and collapsed in tears. I'd wonder how I was blessed by five sweet angels, but still felt empty, broken and scared. Negative thoughts swarmed my mind. I'd grab food to self soothe. I was unhealthy and didn't understand self-care. My children were "my world." I had zero time for myself. I was conditioned to put my own wellness LAST. I was scared and knew no different. Belief in myself, and HAPPINESS, did not exist.

After a health scare, I realized I had to take care of myself, to take care of them. I stepped outside my comfort zone, using belief to rise above fear. Great things happened -- not overnight, of course -- but one small step began my transformation journey, eventually snowballing into where I am today: healthy, fulfilled, happy in mind and body. Living my best life.

Let's talk about you. How do YOU make such a shift when it seems impossible?

It Starts with a Plan!

Create a plan that ensures you reach your destination, and enjoy the journey along the way. Consider the metaphor of taking a trip somewhere. You can choose to travel by plane, car, or rowboat. Imagine a horizontal line from left to right. This line represents your journey. On the left, your plan begins. The right end of the line is your desired outcome. All that matters on this journey is that you move in the "right" direction towards your destination.

You'll be blocked (or slowed down) by speed bumps, rock slides, bad weather, and delayed flights. That's okay! Challenges are part of life. Have focus. Continue moving towards your destination. Understand and evaluate. Do not let anything come between you and your inevitable success.

Your journey is unique. Stay consistent, don't stop, and you WILL get there. Consistency is the key to success:

- CONSISTENCY leads to HABITS.

- HABITS form your daily ACTIONS.

- ACTIONS leads you to SUCCESS.

Developing these consistent patterns elevates your confidence, which has a compound effect that helps you accomplish those goals and arrive at your destination.

To make a change, update your wiring. Override your current thoughts with new and improved data. Change the channel until you find a "channel" that aligns with who you want to be and where you want to go. You may not find the perfect channel on the first click (or maybe ever) but you aren't seeking perfection. You are looking to move one step closer to your chosen destination. Mindshift!

One Decision Away...

You are fortunate. You can choose and design the life you desire. When your intentions and mindset are clear, you are only one decision away from exactly what you want. With every decision, you are either closer or further away from your goal.

> *"Experiences shape our brain matter."*
> *-- Philippa Perry*

Consistent actions, good or bad, create strong connections between neurons. Your brain can make these positive or negative connections at any time.

You can alter negative connections (even if you have had them for years), and shift towards healthy, positive connections.

I know how you feel. I've been where you are. You may not know where to begin or how to change your situation. I've done the research and work, I've had success. I would be happy to take your hand while you travel the road towards your destination.

Today, my life is much different than it once was. I am happy, confident, and found the answer to true health, dropping over 150 pounds. I understand the importance of optimal nutrition for your brain and body. I've studied psychology and our amazing brain, and by putting in the work, was able to positively alter my mindset and my life. I am blessed to give back by coaching others to greatness, and it's been rewarding helping people around the world understand they have a choice, and can make the decision not to settle for less than living their best life.

> *"Change your thoughts and you change your world."*
> *-- Norman Vincent Peale*

It starts with one decision, one step.

Colleen Rekers is the Founder of the One Spark Movement. A life and wellness coach, speaker, writer, and entrepreneur, who also runs a successful Isagenix business. Her training, education, research, and life experience have catapulted her into the life, wellness, personal development arenas.

Claim your free Mindshift Map to enable YOU to Level Up Your Life, online at **LevelUpYourLifeWithColleen.com.** This exercise will help you flush through and identify the state of your current mindset. You'll pinpoint the areas that need work, to enhance your life. Learn more on how Colleen Rekers can help you live your best life at ColleenRekers.com.

Level 11: Failure... Recover From Mistakes to Awaken Your Compassion by Suzy Prudden

Level yourself up to failure. What?! Why shouldn't you Level Up to Success, Brilliance, Wealth, Beauty, Health? Why FAILURE? Without Failure you cannot have Success, Brilliance, Wealth, Beauty, Health, or WHATEVER you strive for. Failure is one of the most important tools you are given in life to achieve your goals, success, and future.

You are told that failure is a bad thing. In school, to fail is to be bad. But without failure you do not learn. You we can skim through life getting things done and making things happen but to endure a failure and get back up again and rebuild? That takes power. Recovering from failure makes you stronger, wiser, more conscious, more aware, more determined, and much more compassionate. I'm sure there are many other words I could fill in here. Perhaps you can add your own!

Millions

I've made and lost millions (I prefer MAKING millions). I've been a household name and I've been invisible. As this relates to you, what does it take to have those multiple careers, successes, and failures, that you'll experience in your life journey? It takes GRIT!

I was a blessed child with a happy, loving, wealthy childhood. I was an athlete and attended a school that passed me to the next grade whether I learned anything or not. I was skiing at age 2, rock climbing at age 6, swimming at 7, riding at 7, a gymnast and a dancer. By age 12 I had eight serious (knock out) concussions and could not read or do math. I changed schools. I was told I wasn't stupid but failed 7th grade with straight F's. No one knew I had a brain injury. I'm glad they didn't or I would have been pigeonholed into a category and labeled something. In my case, I went to a great boarding school (North Country School in Lake Placid, New York), where I participated in all my favorite activities. Teachers were patient in bringing me up to speed.

A Blessing in Disguise

Failing 7th grade with straight F's was one of my greatest successes. At this fabulous boarding school, I met the children of the wealthiest families in America, I excelled at my strengths and learned skills to take me to the next level.

Those were the early years. My mother told me I couldn't date the boy I was dating to college so I ran away and got married. I had to support him because he went back to school. I started a fitness school because I was the daughter of the nation's leading fitness authority, Bonnie Prudden (launched by Eisenhower as President of the Physical Fitness and Sports Council) and that's what I knew how to do. It was tough. It was in 1965, when there were maybe two other fitness schools in New York City. We had a baby, of course! Now I had a husband in school, a business AND a baby! I couldn't make it work. I was failing.

I got creative. I taught toddler classes that nobody did at the time and mother-child lessons. Note, this was in the 60's. One of the mothers asked me if she could invite a reporter friend of hers to come see the class. Not knowing anything about Public Relations or the press, I agreed, and did nothing special to prepare. The reporter brought a photographer, stayed for both classes, and interviewed me. Three weeks later, The New York Times printed a three-fourths page article with three photos. Within 3 days, class attendance skyrocketed from 10 students to 75. Suzy Prudden Studios was launched. The day the reporter visited, I wasn't sure if I could pay my rent that month!

My Career Climbed

We had easy years and difficult years. Failure was always just around the corner. In 1976, I didn't know there was a recession. I just couldn't understand why we couldn't make enough money. I saw Olga Korbet at the Olympics, on the balance beam lying on her stomach bringing her legs up over her back to touch her toes above her head (over her back, not over her stomach). I thought, "We have to start a gymnastics program." I had been a gymnast in school in Germany but knew nothing. I hired a gymnastics coach, placed ads on the local upper-west side papers, and all of a sudden we had a full-swing gymnastics program in a 1000 square-foot space. That saved the company. We had been failing, but creativity saved the day.

Failure is your gift, if you choose to view it that way. You can choose to say "boo-hoo" but that will only keep you where you don't want to be. And yes, it's NOT always easy.

Get Out!

At this point, I was in my 30's, with a condo I purchased on the Upper West Side, a house in East Hampton, Long Island, and a son in a private school. I was miserable!

I had my own TV Show on NBC. I had been a Fitness Reporter for The Today Show. I had articles written about being in every major publication in New York. I had completed several promotional tours for books I'd written with my husband. It LOOKED like a good life. I was miserable.

I do not believe in the statement, "You made your bed, now lie in it." I believe, "If you don't like the bed, get out" -- which is what I did! I divorced my husband, sold my business, sent my son to boarding school (it saved my life, I was pretty sure it would help him in his – I wasn't a stable mother at the time -- and it did!) and began researching the mind.

I moved to California, met and became friends with Louise Hay and we created a project together: a book and videotape series called, "MetaFitness: Your Thoughts Taking Shape." This venture landed me a guest spot on Oprah. That was a HEADY experience. I didn't know how to handle it. I didn't have a team or program. I THOUGHT I knew what I was doing, but I was stupid and arrogant. Eight months after being on Oprah, I was homeless. I lost it all again this time.

This is Where the Rubber Met the Road

This was the worst loss I've ever experienced. I destroyed my life, reputation, assets and self-esteem. But I had to keep going! I used to make $5,000 a day, and had to take a $10 an hour job. I did what I had to do. I packed my belongings, put everything in storage and went on the road.

Gary Zukov, author of "The Seat of the Soul," asked, "How did you do that?" My response, "I fell back into the arms of God." That's how the gift of Failure works in your life. When you fail, and I have done so many times, I've always trusted that God, The Force, Yoda or that "higher power" in some form, exists. Trust that there is a DIVINE path to follow. You will pass beyond failure to your purpose.

Age 40. Broke with no known skills. I was an incredible teacher, speaker, writer, workshop leader, with no idea of who I was. Famous, completely broke and homeless. I've always had a great place to stay, supportive friends, with no idea what else to do but rebuild. I started anew... again!

Shame was the worst part of the experience. I had it all and I blew it. Time to get creative!

My sister and I created a multi-million dollar publishing company 5 years ago (I'm now 76) and we are starting to get noticed in airports, Staples, Target, and we are back "in the chips." My sister (age 80) informed me she's retiring this month. I must figure out how to run the company alone.

See the pattern? It's time to call upon God and my best self AGAIN, as always! This is also what YOU must do in order to continue and level up.

Suzy Prudden from IttyBittyPublishing.com *is the author of twelve books, including the best selling, Suzy Prudden's Spot Reducing, Itty Bitty Weight Loss Book, MetaFitness: Your Thoughts Taking Shape, and Change Your Mind, Change Your Body. She's been a guest expert on over 1,000 radio and television shows including The Today Show, Good Morning America, and Oprah, who said of Suzy, "In order to heal your relationship with your body, you have to go inside. The answers are all in Suzy Prudden's book, Change Your Mind, Change Your Body."*

Level 12: Action... Take Calculated Risks, Experiment & Simplify by Dr. Mike Woo-Ming

In medicine, there has been a growing epidemic of physician burnout. I know this situation all too well. Years ago, I was a primary care physician, working 50 to 60 hours per week. I was increasingly frustrated with my job. I had no autonomy. I've always loved medicine, but I didn't love what medicine was doing to ME.

Complicating the matter, my son was diagnosed with autism. I asked to switch to part-time hours in order to devote more time to my family, but I was told this was not an option. I quit.

However, I didn't quit instantly! I explored different streams of revenue, and by creating an online business, I used my expertise to help others AND get paid.

The Internet

I had MANY doubts and fears. No training existed that specifically applied to me, a medical doctor. I sought mentors and befriended "internet multimillionaire" colleagues.

I already worked more than full-time. Getting another job was not an option. The internet allowed me to create products and services that served customers, perhaps thousands of miles away.

It took me over 6 months to write my first "health" e-book. I created a webpage and inserted an order button. The first month, I only sold five copies at $20 each.

Some would say, "What a failure!" However, that first $100 was life-changing. I earned that money in my sleep. I repeated that process to validate more products and services. I had information I could share with the world -- and get paid for it! This gave me the opportunity to develop PASSIVE revenue streams.

Multiple Streams of Income

This led to my own full-blown business. I started a consultancy, marketing agency, and co-owned a software company. Eventually I returned to medicine, and opened my own wellness clinic and med spa.

This was ALSO new territory for me, but I followed the same journey! I found successful medical practice owners, who knew the ins and outs of marketing and attracted new patients, which allowed me to overcome MANY small business hurdles.

I share this knowledge with my own students. Today, I help healthcare professionals, mostly physicians, who want to develop their own business with an emphasis on online ventures, as well as those who want to develop brick and mortar cash-based practices. I show them that they have the ability to start their own business and give them the direction and confidence for them to achieve these goals.

Low-Hanging Fruit

Medical professionals have the knowledge and expertise to engage in entrepreneurial ventures, and I help to give them the confidence and guidance to achieve these goals. Doctors are told they are "bad at business." I don't believe that. Marketing and sales are skills that can be learned and mastered. Apply the correct insight and desire, and anything is possible.

I work with medical professionals -- who are often in a different situation than most entrepreneurs.

These people work many hours, and make a decent income, BUT they don't have the time or energy to create a second income stream. They have very little business training. I teach outsourcing, leveraging expertise, and transforming that into mass-consumable form. Pursue low-hanging fruit, already-successful markets, instead of trying to create the next Uber or PayPal.

Evergreen Income & Model What Works

I know almost every method of making money online. The ideal methods are those that are "evergreen" -- they continue to generate SUSTAINABLE income over time.

Consider a consulting side business, ESPECIALLY if you are a medical professional. This income stream is independent of the hours you have available and can be run from any location.

Research for a few hours to find what is ALREADY successful. It would be "fun" to create the next Tesla, but you most likely don't have millions of dollars for research and development. Find your own way into that existing market.

You have your own experiences, knowledge, and solutions. I achieved success only AFTER I realized that successful people already existed. I only needed to apply my own unique "spin" on MY solution.

For example, Amazon lists the top bestselling books in every category. Etsy shows how well particular handcrafted items sell. eBay displays their most popular items. Some markets sell again and again, and will continue to sell!

A market with zero competitors is a sign of DANGER. You might have expertise in underwater basket weaving, but if no products exist in that market, there is no money to be made.

Invest in Yourself

Doctors tend to have control issues. It's "my way or the highway!" I swallowed my ego. A smarter path was to find mentors, and model their successes. "Success leaves clues!"

I have met some amazing students who have done great things. One physician was burnt out and now has the most successful weight-loss clinic in her city. I've worked with individuals who acquired multimillion dollar businesses that run from a laptop.

Unfortunately, others never take action, or have never started -- not because of a lack of tools. They don't have the confidence or motivation to change their mindset. Life gets in the way, and they let distraction win.

Be Accountable and Commit

When starting a business, forget about being "risk-averse." There are no guarantees in life.

Find the discipline and focus to get to where you want to go. Get clear on your financial (and other) reasons to start your business. The unexpected CAN happen. However, every failure brings you one step closer to success. Your ability to overcome those inevitable challenges is what turns failure into success.

The most successful clients I work with are those who are ready for change. They're open to my suggestions. These people are ready to do what it takes to become successful -- leaving no stone unturned to get to that goal. If YOU are ready to invest in your own success, there is no better time than the present.

Those times I failed to make progress, I was the one at fault, NOT the coach or consultant.

The definition of insanity is when you do the same thing again and again, hoping for different results. Early in my career, I met with doctors who were unhappy about their circumstances but didn't do anything to change their situation. They were miserable towards themselves, their families, friends, and patients. No one benefits in that situation. I didn't want to take that same path.

Now, I have the freedom to do what I want and work when I want, and not to be shackled by other institutions, or to bosses that could bring me down. This has given me more time for myself and more time to spend with my friends and family.

The Shortcut to Success

It's not roses all the time, but having the time to do what I want has made all the difference. If you want a change, having a mentor is a shortcut to success. If you're not ready to start something, what other options are available? If you're unable to consider other options, find a mentor that aligns with your beliefs and goals.

I don't often have new clients, but if you're a medical professional looking to make a change, the best way for us to get started is to go to my website at BootstrapMD.com to see my availability and sign up for a consultation. Let's have a conversation about your entrepreneurial endeavors to see if there are areas to which I can give clarity. I'm looking forward to talking to you soon.

Mike Woo-Ming MD MPH is a medical entrepreneur and marketing strategist who oversees the development and growth of several multi-million dollar online companies.

He's the CEO of Executive Medical (ExecMed.org), which specializes in age management, medical weight loss and aesthetics in the San Diego suburbs, and co-owns many more cash-based practices, including weight loss, regenerative medicine, and med spa services in Southern California. His goal is to help 1000 doctors live life on their own terms. He's the founder of BootstrapMD.com, providing career consulting and mentoring for physician entrepreneurs for over a decade.

About Robert Plank, Compilation Publisher

Robert Plank is an online business coach who would like to help you manage your time, get your life back, and simplify your daily activities.

Using systems, checklists, and templates, you can write a book within an hour and become a published author in 12 hours. You can setup a membership site in one day, create a blog or podcast in 5 minutes or less, and so much more.

- More about this book: BookLevelUp.com
- Podcast: MarketerOfTheDay.com

Conclusion: What's Next?

What ah-ha's did you have after absorbing some of these stories? Did any particular expert's story or advice stand out for you?

Did you notice any "common threads" in the success stories you experienced?

Perhaps you noticed something simple, for example, that these experts have all experienced multiple, massive setbacks. Most used some form of visualization, imagination, positive thinking, mindset tools, and mentorship to get things done. Surprisingly, quite a few mentioned the ADDICTIVENESS of their business and success in order to continue making progress.

What is the next level for you? I'm hoping that after finding out that your dreams are possible, that you are not going through this alone. MANY people have been where you are (in more ways than one).

Finally, if you enjoyed this book, we would all appreciate an honest review when you go to:

BookLevelUp.com/amazon